PENGUIN BOOKS — GREAT IDEAS

An Image of Africa and *The Trouble with Nigeria*

D1332674

Chinua Achebe
(born 1930)

Chinua Achebe

An Image of Africa and
The Trouble with Nigeria

PENGUIN BOOKS — GREAT IDEAS

PENGUIN BOOKS

Published by the Penguin Group
Penguin Books Ltd, 80 Strand, London wc2r orl, England
Penguin Group (USA) Inc., 375 Hudson Street, New York, New York 10014, USA
Penguin Group (Canada), 90 Eglinton Avenue East, Suite 700, Toronto, Ontario,
Canada m4p 2y3 (a division of Pearson Penguin Canada Inc.)
Penguin Ireland, 25 St Stephen's Green, Dublin 2, Ireland (a division of Penguin Books Ltd)
Penguin Group (Australia), 250 Camberwell Road, Camberwell, Victoria 3124, Australia
(a division of Pearson Australia Group Pty Ltd)
Penguin Books India Pvt Ltd, 11 Community Centre, Panchsheel Park,
New Delhi – 110 017, India
Penguin Group (NZ), 67 Apollo Drive, Rosedale, North Shore 0632, New Zealand
(a division of Pearson New Zealand Ltd)
Penguin Books (South Africa) (Pty) Ltd, 24 Sturdee Avenue, Rosebank, Johannesburg 2196,
South Africa

Penguin Books Ltd, Registered Offices: 80 Strand, London wc2r orl, England

www.penguin.com

'An Image of Africa' was originally given as the second Chancellor's Lecture at the
University of Massachusetts, Amherst, February 1975; later published in the
Massachusetts Review, vol. 18, no. 4, winter 1977, Amherst.
'The Trouble with Nigeria' first published by Fourth Dimension Publishing Co. Ltd 1983
and first published by Heinemann Educational Books 1984
In Canada this book is published with the permission of Anchor Canada
Additional works by Chinua Achebe are published in Canada by Doubleday Canada,
a division of Random House of Canada Limited
This selection published in Penguin Books 2010

010

Copyright © Chinua Achebe, 1977, 1983

Set in 11/13 pt Dante MT Std
Typeset by TexTech International

Printed and bound in Great Britain by Clays Ltd, Elcograf S.p.A.

isbn: 978-0-141-19258-1

www.greenpenguin.co.uk

MIX
Paper from
responsible sources
FSC® C018179

Penguin Books is committed to a sustainable
future for our business, our readers and our planet.
This book is made from Forest Stewardship
Council™ certified paper.

Contents

An Image of Africa: Racism in Conrad's Heart of Darkness

In the fall of 1974 I was walking one day from the English Department at the University of Massachusetts to a parking lot. It was a fine autumn morning such as encouraged friendliness to passing strangers. Brisk youngsters were hurrying in all directions, many of them obviously freshmen in their first flush of enthusiasm. An older man going the same way as I turned and remarked to me how very young they came these days. I agreed. Then he asked me if I was a student too. I said no, I was a teacher. What did I teach? African literature. Now that was funny, he said, because he knew a fellow who taught the same thing, or perhaps it was African *history*, in a certain community college not far from here. It always surprised him, he went on to say, because he never had thought of Africa as having that kind of stuff, you know. By this time I was walking much faster. 'Oh well,' I heard him say finally, behind me: 'I guess I have to take your course to find out.'

A few weeks later I received two very touching letters from high school children in Yonkers, New York, who – bless their teacher – had just read *Things Fall Apart*. One of them was particularly happy to learn about the customs and superstitions of an African tribe.

I propose to draw from these rather trivial encounters rather heavy conclusions which at first sight might seem somewhat out of proportion to them. But only, I hope, at first sight.

The young fellow from Yonkers, perhaps partly on account of his age, but I believe also for much deeper and more serious reasons, is obviously unaware that the life of his own tribesmen in Yonkers, New York, is full of odd customs and superstitions and, like everybody else in his culture, imagines that he needs a trip to Africa to encounter those things.

The other person being fully my own age could not be excused on the grounds of his years. Ignorance might be a more likely reason; but here again I believe that something more wilful than a mere lack of information was at work. For did not that erudite British historian and Regius Professor at Oxford, Hugh Trevor-Roper, also pronounce that African history did not exist?

If there is something in these utterances more than youthful inexperience, more than a lack of factual knowledge, what is it? Quite simply it is the desire – one might indeed say the need – in Western psychology to set Africa up as a foil to Europe, as a place of negations at once remote and vaguely familiar, in comparison with which Europe's own state of spiritual grace will be manifest.

This need is not new; which should relieve us all of considerable responsibility and perhaps make us even willing to look at this phenomenon dispassionately. I have neither the wish nor the competence to embark on the exercise with the tools of the social and biological sciences but do so more simply in the manner of a novelist responding to one famous book of European fiction: Joseph Conrad's *Heart of Darkness*, which better than any other work that I know displays that Western desire and need which I have just referred to. Of course there are whole libraries of books devoted to the same purpose but most of them are so obvious and so crude that few people worry about them today. Conrad, on the other hand, is undoubtedly one of the great stylists of modern fiction and a good story-teller into the bargain. His contribution therefore falls automatically into a different class – permanent literature – read and taught and constantly evaluated by serious academics. *Heart of Darkness* is indeed so secure today that a leading Conrad scholar has numbered it 'among the half-dozen greatest short novels in the English language.' I will return to this critical opinion in due course because it may seriously modify my earlier suppositions about who may or may not be guilty in some of the matters I will now raise.

Heart of Darkness projects the image of Africa as 'the other world,' the antithesis of Europe and therefore of civilization, a place where man's vaunted intelligence and refinement are finally mocked by triumphant bestiality. The book opens on the River Thames, tranquil, resting peacefully 'at the decline of day after ages of good service done to the race that peopled its banks.' But the actual story will take place on the River Congo, the very antithesis of the Thames. The River Congo is quite decidedly not a River Emeritus. It has rendered no service and enjoys no old-age pension. We are told that 'going up that river was like travelling back to the earliest beginning of the world.'

Is Conrad saying then that these two rivers are very different, one good, the other bad? Yes, but that is not the real point. It is not the differentness that worries Conrad but the lurking hint of kinship, of common ancestry. For the Thames too 'has been one of the dark places of the earth.' It conquered its darkness, of course, and is now in daylight and at peace. But if it were to visit its primordial relative, the Congo, it would run the terrible risk of hearing grotesque echoes of its own forgotten darkness, and falling victim to an avenging recrudescence of the mindless frenzy of the first beginnings.

These suggestive echoes comprise Conrad's famed evocation of the African atmosphere in *Heart of Darkness*. In the final consideration, his method amounts to no more than a steady, ponderous, fake-ritualistic repetition of two antithetical sentences, one about silence and the other about frenzy. We can inspect samples of this on pages 103 and 105 of the New American Library edition: (a) 'It was the stillness of an implacable force brooding over an inscrutable intention' and (b) 'The steamer toiled along slowly on the edge of a black and incomprehensible frenzy.' Of course, there is a judicious change of adjective from time to time, so that instead of 'inscrutable,' for example, you might have 'unspeakable,' even plain 'mysterious,' etc., etc.

The eagle-eyed English critic F. R. Leavis drew attention long ago to Conrad's 'adjectival insistence upon inexpressible and incomprehensible mystery.' That insistence must not be dismissed lightly, as many Conrad critics have tended to do, as a mere stylistic flaw; for it raises serious questions of artistic good faith. When a writer while pretending to record scenes, incidents, and their impact is in reality engaged in inducing hypnotic stupor in his readers through a bombardment of emotive words and other forms of trickery, much more has to be at stake than stylistic felicity. Generally, normal readers are well armed to detect and resist such underhand activity. But Conrad chose his subject well – one which was guaranteed not to put him in conflict with the psychological predisposition of his readers or raise the need for him to contend with their resistance. He chose the role of purveyor of comforting myths.

The most interesting and revealing passages in *Heart of Darkness* are, however, about people. I must crave the indulgence of my reader to quote almost a whole page from about the middle of the story when representatives of Europe in a steamer going down the Congo encounter the denizens of Africa:

> We were wanderers on a prehistoric earth, on an earth that wore the aspect of an unknown planet. We could have fancied ourselves the first of men taking possession of an accursed inheritance, to be subdued at the cost of profound anguish and of excessive toil. But suddenly, as we struggled round a bend, there would be a glimpse of rush walls, of peaked grass-roofs, a burst of yells, a whirl of black limbs, a mass of hands clapping, of feet stamping, of bodies swaying, of eyes rolling, under the droop of heavy and motionless foliage. The steamer toiled along slowly on the edge of the black and incomprehensible frenzy. The prehistoric man was cursing us, praying to us, welcoming us – who could tell? We were cut off from the comprehension of our surroundings; we glided past like phantoms, wondering and secretly appalled, as sane men would be before an enthusiastic outbreak in a madhouse. We could not understand because we were too

far and could not remember because we were travelling in the night of first ages, of those ages that are gone, leaving hardly a sign – and no memories.

The earth seemed unearthly. We are accustomed to look upon the shackled form of a conquered monster, but there – there you could look at a thing monstrous and free. It was unearthly, and the men were – No, they were not inhuman. Well, you know, that was the worst of it – this suspicion of their not being inhuman. It would come slowly to one. They howled and leaped, and spun, and made horrid faces; but what thrilled you was just the thought of their humanity – like yours – the thought of your remote kinship with this wild and passionate uproar. Ugly. Yes, it was ugly enough; but if you were man enough you would admit to yourself that there was in you just the faintest trace of a response to the terrible frankness of that noise, a dim suspicion of there being a meaning in it which you – you so remote from the night of first ages – could comprehend.

Herein lies the meaning of *Heart of Darkness* and the fascination it holds over the Western mind: 'What thrilled you was just the thought of their humanity – like yours . . . Ugly.'

Having shown us Africa in the mass, Conrad then zeros in, half a page later, on a specific example, giving us one of his rare descriptions of an African who is not just limbs or rolling eyes:

> And between whiles I had to look after the savage
> who was fireman. He was an improved specimen;

he could fire up a vertical boiler. He was there below me, and, upon my word, to look at him was as edifying as seeing a dog in a parody of breeches and a feather hat, walking on his hind legs. A few months of training had done for that really fine chap. He squinted at the steam gauge and at the water gauge with an evident effort of intrepidity – and he had filed his teeth, too, the poor devil, and the wool of his pate shaved into queer patterns, and three ornamental scars on each of his cheeks. He ought to have been clapping his hands and stamping his feet on the bank, instead of which he was hard at work, a thrall to strange witchcraft, full of improving knowledge.

As everybody knows, Conrad is a romantic on the side. He might not exactly admire savages clapping their hands and stamping their feet but they have at least the merit of being in their place, unlike this dog in a parody of breeches. For Conrad, things being in their place is of the utmost importance.

'Fine fellows – cannibals – in their place,' he tells us pointedly. Tragedy begins when things leave their accustomed place, like Europe leaving its safe stronghold between the policeman and the baker to take a peep into the heart of darkness.

Before the story takes us into the Congo basin proper we are given this nice little vignette as an example of things in their place:

Now and then a boat from the shore gave one a momentary contact with reality. It was paddled by black fellows.

You could see from afar the white of their eyeballs glistening. They shouted, sang; their bodies streamed with perspiration; they had faces like grotesque masks – these chaps; but they had bone, muscle, a wild vitality, an intense energy of movement, that was as natural and true as the surf along their coast. They wanted no excuse for being there. They were a great comfort to look at.

Towards the end of the story Conrad lavishes a whole page quite unexpectedly on an African woman who has obviously been some kind of mistress to Mr Kurtz and now presides (if I may be permitted a little liberty) like a formidable mystery over the inexorable imminence of his departure:

She was savage and superb, wild-eyed and magnificent. . . . She stood looking at us without a stir and like the wilderness itself, with an air of brooding over an inscrutable purpose.

This Amazon is drawn in considerable detail, albeit of a predictable nature, for two reasons. First, she is in her place and so can win Conrad's special brand of approval; and second, she fulfils a structural requirement of the story; a savage counterpart to the refined, European woman who will step forth to end the story:

She came forward, all in black with a pale head, floating toward me in the dusk. She was in mourning . . . She took both my hands in hers and murmured, 'I had heard you were coming' . . . She had a mature capacity for fidelity, for belief, for suffering.

The difference in the attitude of the novelist to these two women is conveyed in too many direct and subtle ways to need elaboration. But perhaps the most significant difference is the one implied in the author's bestowal of human expression to the one and the withholding of it from the other. It is clearly not part of Conrad's purpose to confer language on the 'rudimentary souls' of Africa. In place of speech they made 'a violent babble of uncouth sounds.' They 'exchanged short grunting phrases' even among themselves. But most of the time they were too busy with their frenzy. There are two occasions in the book, however, when Conrad departs somewhat from his practice and confers speech, even English speech, on the savages. The first occurs when cannibalism gets the better of them:

> 'Catch 'im,' he snapped, with a bloodshot widening of his eyes and a flash of sharp white teeth – 'catch 'im to us.' 'To you, eh?' I asked; 'what would you do with them?' 'Eat 'im!' he said curtly.

The other occasion was the famous announcement: 'Mistah Kurtz – he dead.'

At first sight these instances might be mistaken for unexpected acts of generosity from Conrad. In reality they constitute some of his best assaults. In the case of the cannibals the incomprehensible grunts that had thus far served them for speech suddenly proved inadequate for Conrad's purpose of letting the European glimpse the unspeakable craving in their hearts. Weighing the necessity for consistency in the portrayal of the dumb brutes against the sensational advantages of securing their conviction by clear, unambiguous evidence issuing out of their own mouths, Conrad chose the latter. As for the announcement of Mr Kurtz's death by the 'insolent black head in the doorway,' what better or more appropriate *finis* could be written to the horror story of that wayward child of civilization who wilfully had given his soul to the powers of darkness and 'taken a high seat amongst the devils of the land' than the proclamation of his physical death by the forces he had joined?

It might be contended, of course, that the attitude to the African in *Heart of Darkness* is not Conrad's but that of his fictional narrator, Marlow, and that far from endorsing it Conrad might indeed be holding it up to irony and criticism. Certainly, Conrad appears to go to considerable pains to set up layers of insulation between himself and the moral universe of his story. He has, for example, a narrator behind a narrator. The primary narrator is Marlow, but his account is given to us through the filter of a second, shadowy person. But if Conrad's intention is to draw a cordon sanitaire between himself and the moral and psychological *malaise* of his narrator, his care seems to me totally wasted because he neglects to hint, clearly and adequately, at an alternative frame of reference by which we may judge the actions and opinions of his characters. It would not have been beyond Conrad's power to make that provision if he had thought it necessary. Conrad seems to me to approve of Marlow, with only minor reservations – a fact reinforced by the similarities between their two careers.

Marlow comes through to us not only as a witness of truth, but one holding those advanced and humane views appropriate to the English liberal tradition which required all Englishmen of decency to be deeply shocked by atrocities in Bulgaria or the Congo of King Leopold of the Belgians or wherever.

Thus, Marlow is able to toss out such bleeding-heart sentiments as these:

> They were all dying slowly – it was very clear. They were not enemies, they were not criminals, they were nothing earthly now – nothing but black shadows of disease and starvation, lying confusedly in the greenish gloom. Brought from all the recesses of the coast in all the legality of time contracts, lost in uncongenial surroundings, fed on unfamiliar food, they sickened, became inefficient, and were then allowed to crawl away and rest.

The kind of liberalism espoused here by Marlow/ Conrad touched all the best minds of the age in England, Europe and America. It took different forms in the minds of different people but almost always managed to sidestep the ultimate question of equality between white people and black people. That extraordinary missionary Albert Schweitzer, who sacrificed brilliant careers in music and theology in Europe for a life of service to Africans in much the same area as Conrad writes about, epitomizes the ambivalence. In a comment which has often been quoted Schweitzer says: 'The African is indeed my brother but my junior brother.' And so he proceeded to build a hospital appropriate to the needs of junior brothers with standards of hygiene reminiscent of medical practice in the days before the germ theory of disease came into being. Naturally he became a sensation in Europe and America. Pilgrims flocked, and I believe still flock even after he has passed on, to witness the prodigious miracle in Lambaréné, on the edge of the primeval forest.

Conrad's liberalism would not take him quite as far as Schweitzer's, though. He would not use the word 'brother' however qualified; the farthest he would go was 'kinship.' When Marlow's African helmsman falls down with a spear in his heart he gives his white master one final disquieting look:

> And the intimate profundity of that look he gave me when he received his hurt remains to this day in my memory – like a claim of distant kinship affirmed in a supreme moment.

It is important to note that Conrad, careful as ever with his words, is concerned not so much about 'distant kinship' as about someone *laying a claim* on it. The black man lays a claim on the white man which is well-nigh intolerable. It is the laying of this claim which frightens and at the same time fascinates Conrad, 'the thought of their humanity – like yours . . . Ugly.'

The point of my observations should be quite clear by now, namely that Joseph Conrad was a thoroughgoing racist. That this simple truth is glossed over in criticisms of his work is due to the fact that white racism against

Africa is such a normal way of thinking that its manifestations go completely unremarked. Students of *Heart of
Darkness* will often tell you that Conrad is concerned not
so much with Africa as with the deterioration of one
European mind caused by solitude and sickness. They
will point out to you that Conrad is, if anything, less
charitable to the Europeans in the story than he is to the
natives, that the point of the story is to ridicule Europe's
civilizing mission in Africa. A Conrad student informed
me in Scotland that Africa is merely a setting for the dis-
integration of the mind of Mr Kurtz.

Which is partly the point. Africa as setting and back-
drop which eliminates the African as human factor. Africa
as a metaphysical battlefield devoid of all recognizable
humanity, into which the wandering European enters at
his peril. Can nobody see the preposterous and perverse
arrogance in thus reducing Africa to the role of props
for the break-up of one petty European mind? But that is
not even the point. The real question is the dehumanization of Africa and Africans which this age-long attitude
has fostered and continues to foster in the world. And
the question is whether a novel which celebrates this
dehumanization, which depersonalizes a portion of the
human race, can be called a great work of art. My answer
is: No, it cannot. I do not doubt Conrad's great talents.
Even *Heart of Darkness* has its memorably good passages
and moments:

> The reaches opened before us and closed behind, as if
> the forest had stepped leisurely across the water to bar
> the way for our return.

Its exploration of the minds of the European characters is often penetrating and full of insight. But all that has been more than fully discussed in the last fifty years. His obvious racism has, however, not been addressed. And it is high time it was!

Conrad was born in 1857, the very year in which the first Anglican missionaries were arriving among my own people in Nigeria. It was certainly not his fault that he lived his life at a time when the reputation of the black man was at a particularly low level. But even after due allowances have been made for all the influences of contemporary prejudice on his sensibility, there remains still in Conrad's attitude a residue of antipathy to black people which his peculiar psychology alone can explain. His own account of his first encounter with a black man is very revealing:

> A certain enormous buck nigger encountered in Haiti fixed my conception of blind, furious, unreasoning rage, as manifested in the human animal to the end of my days. Of the nigger I used to dream for years afterwards.

Certainly Conrad had a problem with niggers. His inordinate love of that word itself should be of interest to psychoanalysts. Sometimes his fixation on blackness is equally interesting, as when he gives us this brief description: 'A black figure stood up, strode on long black legs, waving long black arms' – as though we might expect a black figure striding along on black legs to wave white arms! But so unrelenting is Conrad's obsession.

As a matter of interest, Conrad gives us in *A Personal Record* what amounts to a companion piece to the buck nigger of Haiti. At the age of sixteen Conrad encountered his first Englishman in Europe. He calls him 'my unforgettable Englishman' and describes him in the following manner:

> [his] calves exposed to the public gaze . . . dazzled the
> beholder by the splendour of their marble-like condition
> and their rich tone of young ivory . . . The light of a
> headlong, exalted satisfaction with the world of men . . .
> illumined his face . . . and triumphant eyes. In passing he
> cast a glance of kindly curiosity and a friendly gleam of
> big, sound, shiny teeth . . . his white calves twinkled
> sturdily.

Irrational love and irrational hate jostling together in the heart of that talented, tormented man. But whereas irrational love may at worst engender foolish acts of indiscretion, irrational hate can endanger the life of the community. Naturally, Conrad is a dream for psychoanalytic critics. Perhaps the most detailed study of him in this direction is by Bernard C. Meyer, MD. In his lengthy book, Dr Meyer follows every conceivable lead (and sometime inconceivable ones) to explain Conrad. As an example, he gives us long disquisitions on the significance of hair and hair-cutting in Conrad. And yet not even one word is spared for his attitude to black people. Not even the discussion of Conrad's antisemitism was enough to spark off in Dr Meyer's mind those other dark and explosive thoughts. Which only leads one to surmise that

Western psychoanalysts must regard the kind of racism displayed by Conrad as absolutely normal despite the profoundly important work done by Frantz Fanon in the psychiatric hospitals of French Algeria.

Whatever Conrad's problems were, you might say he is now safely dead. Quite true. Unfortunately, his heart of darkness plagues us still. Which is why an offensive and deplorable book can be described by a serious scholar as 'among the half-dozen greatest short novels in the English language.' And why it is today perhaps the most commonly prescribed novel in twentieth-century literature courses in English departments of American universities.

There are two probable grounds on which what I have said so far may be contested. The first is that it is no concern of fiction to please people about whom it is written. I will go along with that. But I am not talking about pleasing people. I am talking about a book which parades in the most vulgar fashion prejudices and insults from which a section of mankind has suffered untold agonies and atrocities in the past and continues to do so in many ways and many places today. I am talking about a story in which the very humanity of black people is called in question.

Secondly, I may be challenged on the grounds of actuality. Conrad, after all, did sail down the Congo in 1890 when my own father was still a babe in arms. How could I stand up more than fifty years after his death and purport to contradict him? My answer is that as a sensible man I will not accept just any traveller's tales solely on the grounds that I have not made the journey myself. I will not trust the evidence even of a man's very eyes when I suspect them to be as jaundiced as Conrad's. And we also happen to know that Conrad was, in the words of his biographer, Bernard C. Meyer, 'notoriously inaccurate in the rendering of his own history.'

But more important by far is the abundant testimony about Conrad's savages which we could gather if we were so inclined from other sources and which might lead us to think that these people must have had other occupations besides merging into the evil forest or materializing out of it simply to plague Marlow and his dispirited band. For as it happened, soon after Conrad had written his book an event of far greater consequence was taking place in the art world of Europe. This is how Frank Willett, a British art historian, describes it:

> Gauguin had gone to Tahiti, the most extravagant individual act of turning to a non-European culture in the decades immediately before and after 1900, when European artists were avid for new artistic experiences, but it was only about 1904–5 that African art began to make its distinctive impact. One piece is still identifiable; it is a mask that had been given to Maurice Vlaminck in 1905. He records that Derain was 'speechless' and 'stunned' when he saw it, bought it from Vlaminck and in turn showed it to Picasso and Matisse, who were also greatly affected by it. Ambroise Vollard then borrowed it and had it cast in bronze ... The revolution of twentieth century art was under way!

The mask in question was made by other savages living

just north of Conrad's River Congo. They have a name too: the Fang people, and are without a doubt among the world's greatest masters of the sculptured form. The event Frank Willett is referring to marked the beginning of cubism and the infusion of new life into European art that had run completely out of strength.

The point of all this is to suggest that Conrad's picture of the peoples of the Congo seems grossly inadequate even at the height of their subjection to the ravages of King Leopold's International Association for the Civilization of Central Africa.

Travellers with closed minds can tell us little except about themselves. But even those not blinkered, like Conrad, with xenophobia, can be astonishingly blind. Let me digress a little here. One of the greatest and most intrepid travellers of all time, Marco Polo, journeyed to the Far East from the Mediterranean in the thirteenth century and spent twenty years in the court of Kublai Khan in China. On his return to Venice he set down in his book entitled *Description of the World* his impressions of the peoples and places and customs he had seen. But there were at least two extraordinary omissions in his account. He said nothing about the art of printing, unknown as yet in Europe but in full flower in China. He either did not notice it at all or, if he did, failed to see what use Europe could possibly have for it. Whatever the reason, Europe had to wait another hundred years for Gutenberg. But even more spectacular was Marco Polo's omission of any reference to the Great Wall of China, nearly four thousand miles long and already more than one thousand years old at the time of his visit. Again, he may not have seen it; but the Great Wall of China is the only structure built by man which is visible from the moon! Indeed, travellers can be blind.

As I said earlier Conrad did not originate the image of Africa which we find in his book. It was and is the dominant image of Africa in the Western imagination and Conrad merely brought the peculiar gifts of his own mind to bear on it. For reasons which can certainly use close psychological inquiry, the West seems to suffer deep anxieties about the precariousness of its civilization and to have a need for constant reassurance by comparison with Africa. If Europe, advancing in civilization, could cast a backward glance periodically at Africa trapped in primordial barbarity it could say with faith and feeling: There go I but for the grace of God. Africa is to Europe as the picture is to Dorian Gray – a carrier on to whom the master unloads his physical and moral deformities so that he may go forward, erect and immaculate. Consequently, Africa is something to be avoided just as the picture has to be hidden away to safeguard the man's jeopardous integrity. Keep away from Africa, or else! Mr Kurtz of *Heart of Darkness* should have heeded that warning and the prowling horror in his heart would have kept its place, chained to its lair. But he foolishly exposed himself to the wild irresistible allure of the jungle and lo! the darkness found him out.

In my original conception of this essay I had thought to conclude it nicely on an appropriately positive note in which I would suggest from my privileged position in African and Western cultures some advantages the West might derive from Africa once it rid its mind of old prejudices and began to look at Africa not through a haze of distortions and cheap mystifications but quite simply as a continent of people – not angels, but not rudimentary souls either – just people, often highly gifted people and often strikingly successful in their enterprise with life and society. But as I thought more about the stereotype image, about its grip and pervasiveness, about the wilful tenacity with which the West holds it to its heart; when I thought of the West's television and cinema and newspapers, about books read in its schools and out of school, of churches preaching to empty pews about the need to send help to the heathen in Africa, I realized that no easy optimism was possible. And there was in any case something totally wrong in offering bribes to the West in return for its good opinion of Africa. Ultimately the abandonment of unwholesome thoughts must be its own and only reward. Although I have used the word 'wilful' a few times here to characterize the West's view of Africa, it may well be that what is happening at this stage is more akin to reflex action than calculated malice. Which does not make the situation more but less hopeful.

The *Christian Science Monitor*, a paper more enlightened than most, once carried an interesting article written by its Education Editor on the serious psychological and learning problems faced by little children who speak one language at home and then go to school where something else is spoken. It was a wide-ranging article taking in Spanish-speaking children in America, the children of migrant Italian workers in Germany, the quadrilingual phenomenon in Malaysia and so on. And all this while the article speaks unequivocally about language. But then out of the blue sky comes this:

> In London there is an enormous immigration of children who speak Indian or Nigerian dialects, or some other native language.

I believe that the introduction of 'dialects,' which is technically erroneous in the context, is almost a reflex action caused by an instinctive desire of the writer to downgrade the discussion to the level of Africa and India. And this is quite comparable to Conrad's withholding of language from his rudimentary souls. Language is too grand for these chaps; let's give them dialects!

In all this business a lot of violence is inevitably done not only to the image of despised peoples but even to words, the very tools of possible redress. Look at the phrase 'native language' in the *Christian Science Monitor* excerpt. Surely the only *native* language possible in London is Cockney English. But our writer means something else – something appropriate to the sounds Indians and Africans make!

Although the work of redressing which needs to be done may appear too daunting, I believe it is not one day too soon to begin. Conrad saw and condemned the evil of imperial exploitation but was strangely unaware of the racism on which it sharpened its iron tooth. But the victims of racist slander who for centuries have had to live with the inhumanity it makes them heir to have always known better than any casual visitor, even when he comes loaded with the gifts of a Conrad.

The Trouble with Nigeria

1 Where the Problem Lies

The trouble with Nigeria is simply and squarely a failure of leadership. There is nothing basically wrong with the Nigerian character. There is nothing wrong with the Nigerian land or climate or water or air or anything else. The Nigerian problem is the unwillingness or inability of its leaders to rise to the responsibility, to the challenge of personal example which are the hallmarks of true leadership. On the morning after Murtala Muhammed seized power in July 1975 public servants in Lagos were found 'on seat' at seven-thirty in the morning. Even the 'go-slow' traffic that had defeated every solution and defied every regime vanished overnight from the streets! Why? The new ruler's reputation for ruthlessness was sufficient to transform in the course of only one night the style and habit of Nigeria's unruly capital. That the character of one man could establish that quantum change in a people's social behaviour was nothing less than miraculous. But it shows that social miracles *can* happen.

We know, alas, that that transformation was short-lived; it had begun to fade even before the tragic assassination of Murtala Muhammed. In the final analysis a leader's no-nonsense reputation might induce a favourable climate but in order to effect lasting change it must be followed up with a radical programme of social and economic re-organization or at least a well-conceived and consistent agenda of reform which Nigeria stood, and stands, in dire need of.

I am not here recommending ruthlessness as a necessary qualification for Nigerian leadership. Quite on the contrary. What I *am* saying is that Nigeria is not beyond change. I am saying that Nigeria *can* change today if she discovers leaders who have the will, the ability and the vision. Such people are rare in any time or place. But it is the duty of enlightened citizens to lead the way in their discovery and to create an atmosphere conducive to their emergence. If this conscious effort is not made, good leaders, like good money, will be driven out by bad.

Whenever two Nigerians meet, their conversation will sooner of later slide into a litany of our national deficiencies. *The trouble with Nigeria* has become the subject of our small talk in much the same way as the weather is for the English. But there is a great danger in consigning a life-and-death issue to the daily routine of small talk. No one can do much about the weather: we must accept it and live with or under it. But national bad habits are a different matter; we resign ourselves to them at our peril.

The aim of this booklet is to challenge such resignation. It calls on all thoughtful Nigerians to rise up today and reject those habits which cripple our aspiration and inhibit our chances of becoming a modern and attractive country. Nigeria has many thoughtful men and women of conscience, a large number of talented people. Why is it then that all these patriots make so little impact on the life of our nation? Why is it that our corruption, gross inequities, our noisy vulgarity, our selfishness, our ineptitude seem so much stronger than the good influences at work in our society? Why do the good among us seem so helpless while the worst are full of vile energy?

I believe that Nigeria is a nation favoured by Providence. I believe there are individuals as well as nations who, on account of peculiar gifts and circumstances, are commandeered by history to facilitate mankind's advancement. Nigeria is such a nation. The vast human and material wealth with which she is endowed bestows on her a role in Africa and the world which no one else can assume or fulfil. The fear that should nightly haunt our leaders (but does not) is that they may already have betrayed irretrievably Nigeria's high destiny. The countless billions that a generous Providence poured into our national coffers in the last ten years (1972–1982) would have been enough to launch this nation into the middle-rank of developed nations and transformed the lives of our poor and needy. But what have we done with it? Stolen and salted away by people in power and their accomplices. Squandered in uncontrolled importation of all kinds of useless consumer merchandise from every corner of the globe. Embezzled through inflated contracts to an increasing army of party loyalists who have neither the desire nor the competence to execute their contracts. Consumed in the escalating salaries of a grossly overstaffed and unproductive public service. And so on ad infinitum.

Does it ever worry us that history which neither personal wealth nor power can pre-empt will pass terrible judgment on us, pronounce anathema on our names when we have accomplished our betrayal and passed on? We have lost the twentieth century; are we bent on seeing that our children also lose the twenty-first? God forbid!

2 Tribalism

Nothing in Nigeria's political history captures her problem of national integration more graphically than the chequered fortune of the word *tribe* in her vocabulary. *Tribe* has been accepted at one time as a friend, rejected as an enemy at another, and finally smuggled in through the back-door as an accomplice.

In the life-time of many Nigerians who still enjoy an active public career, Nigeria was called 'a mere geographical expression' not only by the British who had an interest in keeping it so, but even by our 'nationalists' when it suited them to retreat into tribe to check their more successful rivals from other parts of the country. As a student in Ibadan I was an eye-witness to that momentous occasion when Chief Obafemi Awolowo 'stole' the leadership of Western Nigeria from Dr Nnamdi Azikiwe in broad daylight on the floor of the Western House of Assembly and sent the great Zik scampering back to the Niger 'whence [he] came.'

Someday when we shall have outgrown tribal politics, or when our children shall have done so, sober historians of the Nigerian nation will see that event as the abortion of a pan-Nigerian vision which, however ineptly, the

NCNC tried to have and to hold. No matter how anyone attempts to explain away that event in retrospect it was the death of a dream-Nigeria in which a citizen could live and work in a place of his choice anywhere, and pursue any legitimate goal open to his fellows; a Nigeria in which an Easterner might aspire to be premier in the West and a Northerner become Mayor of Enugu. That dream-Nigeria suffered a death-blow from Awolowo's 'success' in the Western House of Assembly in 1951. Perhaps it was an unrealistic dream at the best of times, but some young, educated men and women of my generation did dream it.

And though it died, it never fully faded from our consciousness. You could always find idealistic people from every part of Nigeria who were prepared to do battle if anyone (especially European or American) should ask them: *What is your tribe?* 'I am a Nigerian,' they would say haughtily, drawing themselves to their fullest height. Though alive and well *tribe* had an embarrassing odour.

Then a strange thing happened at our independence in 1960. Our national anthem, our very hymn of deliverance from British colonial bondage, was written for us by a British woman who unfortunately had not been properly briefed on the current awkwardness of the word *tribe*. So we found ourselves on independence morning rolling our tongues around the very same trickster godling:

> Though tribe and tongue may differ
> In brotherhood we stand!

It was a most ominous beginning. And not surprisingly

we did not stand too long in brotherhood. Within six years we were standing or sprawling on a soil soaked in fratricidal blood. When it finally ceased to flow, we were ready for a new anthem written this time by ourselves. And we took care to expunge the jinxed word *tribe*. And to be absolutely certain we buried the alien anthem in its own somnolent evangelical hymn juice (concocted incidentally by another British woman, the third in a remarkable line, the first being Lugard's girl-friend who christened us Nigeria) and invoked the natural dance rhythm of our highlife to mark our national rebirth.

But all this self-conscious wish to banish *tribe* has proved largely futile because a word will stay around as long as there is work for it to do. In Nigeria, in spite of our protestations, there *is* plenty of work for *tribe*. Our threatening gestures against it have been premature, half-hearted or plain deceitful.

A Nigerian child seeking admission into a federal school, a student wishing to enter a College or University, a graduate seeking employment in the public service, a businessman tendering for a contract, a citizen applying for a passport, filing a report with the police or seeking access to any of the hundred thousand avenues controlled by the state, will sooner or later fill out a form which requires him to confess his tribe (or less crudely, and more hypocritically, his state of origin).

Intelligent and useful discussion of tribalism is very often thwarted by vagueness. What is tribalism? I will spare you a comprehensive academic definition. For practical purposes let us say that tribalism is *discrimination against a citizen because of his place of birth*.

Everyone agrees that there are manifestations of tribal culture which we cannot condemn; for example, peculiar habits of dress, food, language, music, etc. In fact many of these manifestations are positive and desirable and confer richness on our national culture.

But to prevent a citizen from living or working anywhere in his country, or from participating in the social, political, economic life of the community in which he chooses to live is another matter altogether. Our constitution disallows it even though, like its makers, it manages to say and unsay on certain crucial issues.

Prejudice against 'outsiders' or 'strangers' is an attitude one finds everywhere. But no modern state can lend its support to such prejudice without undermining its own progress and civilization. America, which we copy when it suits us, should provide an excellent example to us in this connection: that although we may not be able to legislate prejudice and bigotry out of the hearts and minds of individual citizens, the state itself and all its institutions must not practice, endorse or condone such habits. Not long ago I was writing a recommendation for a postgraduate student seeking admission into the University of Pittsburgh, USA. The form had the following direction in bold print to recommenders:

Please make no statement which would indicate the applicant's race, creed or national origin.

Defenders of the Nigerian system may point out that the American nation is two hundred years old while Nigeria is only twenty. But don't forget our declared ambition to become an advanced nation in the shortest possible time, preferably by the year 2000.

3 False Image of Ourselves

In June 1979 former Chancellor Helmut Schmidt of West Germany made this comment about his country:

Germany is not a world power; it does not wish to become a world power.

In August of the same year General Olusegun Obasanjo said of Nigeria during his 'Thank You Tour' of Ogun State:

Nigeria will become one of the ten leading nations in the world by the end of the century.

The contrast between these two leaders speaks for itself – a sober, almost self-deprecatory attitude on the one hand and a flamboyant, imaginary self-concept on the other.

One of the commonest manifestations of under-development is a tendency among the ruling elite to live in a world of make-believe and unrealistic expectations. This is the *cargo cult* mentality that anthropologists some-times speak about – a belief by backward people that someday, without any exertion whatsoever on their own part, a fairy ship will dock in their harbour laden with every goody they have always dreamed of possessing.

Listen to Nigerian leaders and you will frequently hear the phrase *this great country of ours.*

Nigeria is *not* a great country. It is one of the most disorderly nations in the world. It is one of the most corrupt, insensitive, inefficient places under the sun. It is one of the most expensive countries and one of those that give least value for money. It is dirty, callous, noisy, ostentatious, dishonest and vulgar. In short, it is among the most unpleasant places on earth!

It is a measure of our self-delusion that we can talk about developing tourism in Nigeria. Only a masochist with an exuberant taste for self-violence will pick Nigeria for a holiday; only a character out of Tutuola seeking to know punishment and poverty at first hand! No, Nigeria may be a paradise for adventurers and pirates, but not tourists.

I once saw a car sticker in Lagos which said LOVE THIS COUNTRY OR LEAVE IT.

The gentle reader of this booklet may feel like the man who displayed that sticker and wonder why I still live in Nigeria. The answer is simple. Nigeria is where God in His infinite wisdom chose to plant me. Therefore I don't consider that I have any right to seek out a more comfortable corner of the world which someone else's intelligence and labour have tidied up. I know enough history to realize that civilization does not fall down from the sky; it has always been the result of people's toil and sweat, the fruit of their long search for order and justice under brave and enlightened leaders.

I also believe that, hopeless as she may seem today, Nigeria is not absolutely beyond redemption. Critical, yes, but not entirely hopeless. But every single day of continued neglect brings her ever closer to the brink of the abyss. To pull her back and turn her around is clearly beyond the contrivance of mediocre leadership. It calls for greatness. Recently the Secretary to the Federal Government was answering a question on an NTA Sokoto programme. 'Nigerians being what they are,' he said, they will seek out means of siphoning away our foreign exchange.

This is hardly fair. Nigerians are what they are only because their leaders are *not* what *they* should be.

4 Leadership, Nigerian-Style

In spite of conventional opinion Nigeria has been less than fortunate in its leadership. A basic element of this misfortune is the seminal absence of intellectual rigour in the political thought of our founding fathers – a tendency to pious materialistic woolliness and self-centred pedestrianism. A perceptive student of Nigerian politics, James Booth, has drawn attention to the poverty of thought exhibited in the biographies of Dr Azikiwe and Chief Awolowo in contrast to the expressions of ideology to be found even in the more informal works of Mboya, Nyerere and Nkrumah!

In a solemn vow made by Azikiwe in 1937 he pledged:

that henceforth I shall utilize my earned income to secure my enjoyment of a high standard of living and also to give a helping hand to the needy.

Obafemi Awolowo was even more forthright about his ambitions:

> I was going to make myself formidable intellectually, morally invulnerable, to make all the money that is possible for a man with my brains and brawn to make in Nigeria.

Thoughts such as these are more likely to produce aggressive millionaires than selfless leaders of their people.

An absence of objectivity and intellectual rigour at the critical moment of a nation's formation is more than an academic matter. It inclines the fledgling state to disorderly growth and mental deficiency.

On Unity and Faith

The most commonly enunciated Nigerian ideal is *unity*. So important is it to us that it stands inscribed on our coat-of-arms and so sacred that the blood of millions of our countrymen, women and children was shed between 1967 and 1970 to uphold it against secessionist forces. I think it was Mr Ukpabi Asika who defined Nigerian unity as 'an absolute good.'

How valid is this notion of unity as an absolute good? Quite clearly it is nonsense. Unity can only be as good as the purpose for which it is desired. Obviously it is good for a group of people to unite to build a school or a hospital or a nation. But supposing a group of other people get together in order to rob a bank. Their unity is deemed undesirable. Indeed lawyers would call their kind of unity by the unflattering name of conspiracy. Therefore we cannot extol the virtues of unity without first satisfying ourselves that the end to which the unity is directed is unimpeachable.

The second ideal which the Nigerian coat-of-arms celebrates is *faith*. Again faith is as good as the object on which it reposes. For religious people faith in God is a desirable way of life; for humanists it is acceptable to believe in the intrinsic worth of man.

But what about faith in money, or faith in talismans and fetish?

So again, faith is all right provided it is to be placed on something acceptable. It cannot be good in itself. Before we are persuaded to have faith we must first ascertain the nature and worth of the receiver of our faith. We must ask the crucial question: Faith in what? just as in the matter of unity we must ask: Unity to what end?

Therefore 'virtues' like *unity* and *faith* are not absolute but conditional on their satisfaction of other purposes. Their social validity depends on the willingness or the ability of citizens to ask the searching question. This calls for a habit of mental rigour, for which, unfortunately, Nigerians are not famous.

But the really interesting question is why were we drawn in the first place to concepts like *unity* and *faith* with their potentialities for looseness? Why did we not think, for example, of such concepts as *Justice* and *Honesty* which cannot be so easily directed to undesirable ends? *Justice* never prompts the question: Justice for what? Neither does Honesty or Truth. Is it possible that as a nation we instinctively chose to extol easy virtues which are amenable to the manipulation of hypocrites, rather than difficult ones which would have imposed the strain of seriousness upon us? And was that one of the legacies of our Founding Fathers?

5 Patriotism

In spite of the tendency of people in power to speak about this great nation of ours there is no doubt that Nigerians are among the world's most unpatriotic people. But this is not because Nigerians are particularly evil or wicked; in fact they are not. It is rather because patriotism, being part of an unwritten social contract between a citizen and the state, cannot exist where the state reneges on the agreement. The state undertakes to organize society in such a way that the citizen can enjoy peace and justice, and the citizen in return agrees to perform his patriotic duties.

In 1978 or 79 General Obasanjo paid an official visit to the University of Nigeria, Nsukka. Of the academic community assembled in the Niger Room of the Continuing Education Centre and which rose respectfully to its feet on his entry General Obasanjo made a totally unexpected demand. He asked them to recite the National Pledge! A few ambiguous mumbles followed, and then stony silence.

'You see,' said the General bristling with hostility, 'You do not even know the National Pledge.' No doubt he saw in this failure an indictable absence of patriotism among a group he had always held with great suspicion.

*

Who is a patriot? He is a person who loves his country. He is not a person who *says* he loves his country. He is not even a person who shouts or swears or recites or sings his love of his country. He is one who *cares* deeply about the happiness and well-being of his country and all its people. Patriotism is an emotion of love directed by a critical intelligence. A true patriot will always demand the highest standards of his country and accept nothing but the best for and from his people. He will be out-spoken in condemnation of their short-comings without giving way to superiority, despair or cynicism. That is my idea of a patriot.

Quite clearly patriotism is not going to be easy or comfortable in a country as badly run as Nigeria is. And this is not made any easier by the fact that no matter how badly a country may be run there will always be some people whose personal, selfish interests are, in the short term at least, well served by the mismanagement and the social inequities. Naturally they will be extremely loud in their adulation of the country and its system, and will be anxious to pass themselves off as patriots and to vilify those who disagree with them as trouble-makers or even traitors. But doomed is the nation which permits such people to define patriotism for it. Their definition would be about as objective as a Rent Act devised by a commit-tee of avaricious landlords, or the encomiums that a col-ony of blood-sucking ticks might be expected to shower upon the bull on whose back they batten. Spurious patri-otism is one of the hallmarks of Nigeria's privileged classes whose generally unearned positions of sudden power and wealth must seem unreal even to themselves.

To lay the ghost of their insecurity they talk patriotically. But their protestation is only mouth-deep; it does not exist in their heads nor in their hearts and certainly not in the work of their hands.

True patriotism is possible only when the people who rule and those under their power have a common and genuine goal of maintaining the dispensation under which the nation lives. This will, in turn, only happen if the nation is ruled justly, if the welfare of all the people rather than the advantage of the few becomes the corner-stone of public policy.

National pledges and pious admonitions administered by the ruling classes or their paid agents are entirely useless in fostering true patriotism. In extreme circumstances of social, economic and political inequities such as we have in Nigeria, pledges and admonitions may even work in the reverse direction and provoke rejection or cynicism and despair. One shining act of bold, selfless leadership at the top, such as unambiguous refusal to be corrupt or tolerate corruption at the fountain of authority, will radiate powerful sensations of well-being and pride through every nerve and artery of national life.

I saw such a phenomenon on two occasions in Tanzania in the 1960s. The first was when news got around (not from the Ministry of Information but on street corners) that President Nyerere after paying his children's school fees had begged his bank to give him a few months' grace on the repayment of the mortgage on his personal house. The other occasion was when he insisted that anyone in his cabinet or party hierarchy who had any kind of business interests must either relinquish them or leave his official or party position. This was no mere technicality of putting the business interest in escrow but giving it up entirely. And many powerful ministers including the formidable leader of TANU Women were forced to leave the cabinet. On these occasions ordinary Tanzanians seemed to walk around, six feet tall. They did not need sermons on patriotism; nor a committee of bishops and emirs to inaugurate a season of ethical revolution for them.

6 Social Injustice and the Cult of Mediocrity

The major objection to the practice of tribalism is that it exposes the citizen to unfair treatment and social injustice. Less advertised but no less damaging to social morality is the advantage which tribalism may confer on mediocrity. But that is not all. Let us take a hypothetical case where two candidates A and B apply to fill a very important and strategic position. A has the right qualification of competence and character but is of the 'wrong' tribe, while B, less qualified, belongs to the 'right' tribe, and so gets the job. A goes away embittered. B throws a party and then messes up the job. The greatest sufferer is the nation itself which has to contain the legitimate grievance of a wronged citizen; accommodate the incompetence of a favoured citizen and, more important and of greater scope, endure a general decline of morale and subversion of efficiency caused by an erratic system of performance and reward.

Social injustice is therefore not only a matter of

morality but also of sheer efficiency and effectiveness. 'We will buy, hire or steal technology,' said one of our ministers. He did not seem to realize that technology was not an assemblage of artefacts stacked conveniently for ease of lifting, but a particular attitude of mind. And it probably never occurred to him that the people from whom he proposed to steal got where they are because they will never hire a man to perform an important task unless he is the best they can find. Nigeria, on the other hand, is a country where it would be difficult to point to *one* important job held by the most competent person we have. I stand to be corrected!

We have displayed a consistent inclination since we assumed management of our own affairs to opt for mediocrity and compromise, to pick a third and fourth eleven to play for us. And the result: we have always failed and will always fail to make it to the world league. Until, that is, we put merit back on the national agenda.

In recent years an editorial in *New Nigerian* could write mockingly about 'God-knows-what-merit.' Ironically it is our new 'intellectual' elite who today debunk merit for immediate sectional advantage, just as some 'nationalist' leaders in the 1950s forsook nationalism in favour of the quick returns of tribalism. But whereas tribalism might win enough votes to install a reactionary jingoist in a tribal ghetto, the cult of mediocrity will bring the wheels of modernization grinding to a halt throughout the land.

Look at our collapsing public utilities, our inefficient and wasteful parastatals and state-owned companies. If you want electricity, you buy your own generator; if you want water, you sink your own bore-hole; if you want to travel, you set up your own airline. One day soon, said a friend of mine, you will have to build your own post office to send your letters!

Many of us who do not travel or who travel only to Europe and America may think that our inability in Nigeria to provide and maintain basic infrastructures and utilities is a common feature of Third World or even African countries. This is not so.

Three years ago I spent two weeks in Upper Volta which is often listed as the poorest or second poorest country in the world, and which perches precariously on the edge of the Sahara Desert. To my utter astonishment there was no power failure throughout my stay in Ougadougou; the taps in my hotel room not only ran all the time but ran with the kind of pressure one sees in Europe and America. My hotel room was modest but impeccably clean; you could use the towel in the bathroom without wondering, as you must do even in four-star Lagos hotels, whether it was washed after the last lodger left. The food was excellent and the waiters were courteous and well-trained. I was not charged the earth or compelled to make a crippling initial deposit.

Of the endless reasons our managers produce to excuse their lack of performance (including NEPA's cobra on transmission lines) the only one that has *prima facie* worth is the alleged 'explosion' of demand. This is usually backed by statistics that you can neither check nor remember. I am certain that if one got *all* the statistics necessary for making proper evaluation one would discover an equal or greater explosion in staff numbers and staff emoluments. In any case who ever heard of a captain of industry grumbling about an expansion in the demand for his product, instead of meeting the challenge joyfully and increasing his profitability?

The problem is *not* any explosion. It is the inevitable paralysis brought on by the cult of mediocrity which we espouse.

I must here quote a brief excerpt from a recent Nigerian editorial:

> He [the Minister of Mines and Power, Ibrahim Hassan] wants us to believe that the generation and supply of electricity is such a complex task that Nigeria cannot fulfil. Several Third World countries with less material resources than Nigeria have managed through their own efforts to provide their people with constant flow of electricity. Why should Nigeria, the oil-rich giant of Africa, be unable to meet such a basic demand of her people.

I have tried to show that the denial of merit is a form of social injustice which can hurt not only the individuals directly concerned but ultimately the entire society. The motive for the original denial may be tribal discrimination as I have tried to show in preceding arguments. But it may also come from sex prejudice, from political, religious or some other partisan consideration, or from corruption and bribery. It is unnecessary to examine these various motives separately; it is sufficient to say that whenever merit is set aside by prejudice of whatever origin, individual citizens as well as the nation itself are victimized.

I must now hasten to add that the question of social justice is wider, much wider, than my analysis hitherto may appear to indicate. I must not leave the matter on the level at which an NPN stalwart recently tried to win electoral support for his party's candidates. His argument was as follows: these two gentlemen are eminently suitable for the governorship ticket; they have more 'connection' than anybody else around; if you need something you only have to approach them and they will either do it for you or give you a piece of paper to give to someone else who will promptly do it.

You could tell right away that the fellow making these recommendations had to be a contractor of a rather limited imagination. It obviously would never cross his mind to wonder what proportion of Anambra citizens were likely to avail themselves of our candidates' universal joints and connection lubricated by their potent pieces of paper! Point zero one per cent, would be my guess.

But when it comes to grabbing, we, the elite of Nigeria, hardly ever consider our numerical insignificance in relation to the share of the national loot which we lay claim to or possess already. Let me make the position quite clear. Dangerous as the denial of merit in the nation's system of choosing and rewarding its hierarchy of public servants can be, the real explosive potential of social injustice in Nigeria does not reside in the narrow jostling among the elite but in the gargantuan disparity of privilege they have created between their tiny class and the vast multitudes of ordinary Nigerians.

The gap between the highest and the lowest paid

public servants in Nigeria is one of the widest in the whole world. Certainly nothing like it occurs in any country worthy of respect. And let it be understood that I am talking about *salary* alone. If we were to add the innumerable perquisites which accrue legitimately to the people at the top such as subsidized housing, free access to fleets of official cars, free shopping sprees abroad, etc. and illegitimate perquisites such as uncontrolled acquisition of state land, procurement of market stalls under fictitious names for rental to genuine traders; even procurement for resale of government-subsidized commodities such as rice, beer, cement, etc. – if we were to add all these 'invisible' emoluments to the salary there would be no word in the dictionary adequate to describe the institutionalized robbery of the common people of Nigeria by their public 'servants.'

Now, this is not a new phenomenon; it certainly was not created by the post-military civilian administration. It might even be called one of the legacies of colonialism. If so we have had more than two decades to correct it; we have failed to do so but rather chosen to multiply the evil ten-fold. We have no excuse whatsoever.

Recently the Shagari administration found it difficult to pay the new national minimum wage which was raised from ₦100.00 per month to ₦120.00. One had thought that the chance would be seized to peg salaries at the top for the next five years or so. But not on your life! You might as well expect landlords to form a national committee for the sole purpose of lowering house rent!

Government financial experts went to work and produced new salary scales which gave *more* money to the people at the top than it gave to the grumbling cadres below. I heard two excellent reasons for this strange move: (a) the percentage increase at the top was *actually* much lower than the percentage increase at the bottom and (b) the total cost to the Treasury of the increases at the bottom was *actually* higher than the 'token' increases at the top.

In his last recorded television interview Mallam Aminu Kano was insistent that leaders must always ask themselves why they are seeking the mandate of the people to rule – what is the purpose of government.

It seems to me that when this purpose is stripped down to its bare bones it will be seen to fall into two parts:

(a) maintenance of peace in the land and
(b) establishment or extension of social justice among the citizens.

These two parts are clearly inter-related; they are in fact two sides of the same coin. Without peace no meaningful social programme can be undertaken; without justice social order is constantly threatened. And the reason is simple. A normal sensible person will wait for his turn if he is sure that the shares will go round; if not he might start a scramble.

Having touched ever so briefly on the social injustice in our public service let us go one step further and attempt to bring into the picture those of our people who exist far below, and untouched by, our minimum wage controversies: the peasant scratching out a living in the deteriorating rural environment, the petty trader with all his wares on his head, the beggar under the fly-over and millions and millions that you cannot even categorize. Twenty of these would be glad any day to be able to share *one* minimum wage packet!

These are the real victims of our callous system, the wretched of the earth. They are largely silent and invisible. They don't appear on front pages; they do not initiate industrial actions. They drink bad water and suffer from all kinds of preventable diseases. There are no hospitals within reach of them; but even if there were they couldn't afford to attend. There may be a school of sorts which their children go to when there is 'free education' and withdraw from when 'levies' are demanded.

The politician may pay them a siren-visit once in four years and promise to *give* them this and that and the other. He never says that what he *gives* is theirs in the first place. The things that are uppermost in their minds are basic, like clean water. The politician agrees; but there is financial constraint now. The plans are drawn by *my* government; water will be flowing by 1986. Meanwhile I give you the most modern television station in Africa. Surely this will make you smile . . .

Dear reader, you may think I over-draw the picture. Let me assure you that I have only sketched in the tip of the iceberg. As a class, you and I and our friends who comprise the elite are incredibly blind. We refuse to see what we do not want to see. That is why we have not brought about the changes which our society must undergo or be written off. We have no option really; if we do not move, we shall be moved. The masses whose name we take in vain are not amused; they do not enjoy their punishment and poverty. We say thoughtlessly that politics is a game of numbers. So it is. The masses own the nation because they have the numbers. And when they move they will do it knowing that God loves them or He would not have made so many of them.

7 *Indiscipline*

Indiscipline pervades our life so completely today that one may be justified in calling it the condition *par excellence* of contemporary Nigerian society. We see and hear and read about indiscipline in the home, in the school, in the public service, in the private sector, in government and in legislative assemblies, on the roads, in the air.

The malaise takes so many different forms – sometimes brutally crude, at other times more subtle – that a comprehensive definition of it would be very difficult. For our present purposes let us say that indiscipline is *a failure or refusal to submit one's desires and actions to the restraints of orderly social conduct in recognition of the rights and desires of others*. The goal of indiscipline is self-interest; its action, the abandonment of self-restraint in pursuit of the goal. (The fact that the action may sometimes defeat the goal is quite another matter.)

Although indiscipline is by definition distinct from lawlessness, the line between the two is often tenuous indeed. For example an undisciplined driver breaks a traffic regulation by overtaking on the side-walk; then commits the criminal act of manslaughter by knocking down and killing a pedestrian.

The danger of indiscipline escalating into lawlessness

is particularly acute when large numbers of people are involved in it; i.e. in situations of mass indiscipline.

There is no provision in the Laws of Nigeria or the Constitution which says that a man who comes first to a public counter should be served before the man who comes later. But our sense of natural justice and our intelligence tell us that it should be so because (a) it is only fair and (b) experience has shown that any other way is liable to create disorder and delay.

It is this sense of fair-play joined to an intelligent application of human experience which acts as a brake on our selfish impulse to shove other people aside and move to the fore.

Discipline does not invite supervision by an external force but is imposed by the individual from within. Indeed discipline is either self-discipline or it is nothing at all. But although society thus appears to leave individuals to their own discretion in the matter of social discipline, this freedom is strictly circumscribed by sanctions of varying severity. It may be no more than a disapproving look; the typical laconic English censure: *it is not done;* or it may be extremely grave like, for instance, social ostracism.

I think that society realizes that given adequate social education the average citizen will come to appreciate that it is in his own interest to uphold discipline. As soon as a sufficient number of citizens understand this, they will supervise their own behaviour and the behaviour of their immediate neighbours. The resulting condition may be called a *climate of discipline*.

Even in such a climate there will always be sporadic incidents of indiscipline because there will always be people who on account of their immaturity, mental incompetence, sheer devilry or even innocent exuberance are unable or unwilling to impose the internal brake of self-discipline on their desires and actions. But in disciplined societies they will remain an eccentric minority.

In Nigeria the position is quite different. An observer of our national scene might well be pardoned if he ran away with the impression that we were a country with an eccentric minority who can restrain themselves and an overwhelming majority who can't! But I believe that although our condition is critical, and getting worse by the day, we still do have a majority, albeit dormant, of self-controlled citizens. I have carefully observed the behaviour of Nigerian drivers in their notorious and regular business of turning a minor hitch in traffic flow into a complete deadlock by racing out of line and blocking every inch of the road. Although a disquietingly large number of drivers do take part in this madness, you will find that a majority of drivers in fact do not. They stay where they are, cursing the country and getting high blood pressure!

But lest we draw too much solace from this fact let us remember that this majority of reasonable citizens are like sane people who in some bizarre and unexplained way find themselves trapped in a dangerous and rowdy madhouse. The lunatics may be outnumbered but they own the place.

Another reason against complacency is that the lunatic fringe spreads daily by recruiting from the borderline of the sane. As the climate of indiscipline settles firmly on the land, the reasonable driver who stays in line begins to look more and more like a dummy, a naive fool who may be doing what the book says but will get nowhere at all because 'this is not Britain or America but Nigeria.'

There is indeed no better place to observe the thrusting indiscipline in Nigerian behaviour than on the roads: frenetic energy, rudeness, noisiness – they are all there in abundance, held in place, as it were, by that vulgar piousness (which we always mistake for piety) in loud inscriptions proclaiming the vehicle owner's trust in God, straight dealing with all men and, therefore, guaranteed safe arrival.

With this safety in his pocket, as it were, he is ready to face any challenge. The driver ahead of him is one such challenge, and must be subdued and put behind, no matter the road situation. The result is there for all to see – the daily, nay hourly, massacre of our citizens often in the most active and productive periods of their lives and in such numbers every year to populate a whole city; an even larger army of maimed and battered survivors; and the nation's colossal outlay in hospital, insurance and other bills. To which record of wholesale waste we must add the cost of the destroyed vehicles, road structures, public utilities and other material resources.

The amazing thing about the Nigerian road today is that there are no traffic regulations and no traffic police. For a start, there is no speed limit. In America where highway motoring is a major national activity, where a driver's licence is not purchased under the counter, where cars are well-built and well-maintained, where no sudden surprises like unfilled pot-holes, abandoned wrecks or stampeding cows lie in wait for the motorist, there is yet a strictly enforced speed limit of fifty-six miles or eighty-eight kilometers per hour. Now, who has ever heard of a car in Nigeria (unless it is crippled by two flat tyres) doing eighty-eight kilometres per hour? At a hundred and fifty kilometres or a hundred and sixty and more, you would still not be the fastest man on *any* Nigerian road. That is nearly *double* the speed Americans permit on their meticulously monitored super highways.

When I see the needless horror and death we bring upon ourselves on the roads I ask myself: How can intelligent beings do this to themselves? I think there can be only one answer: We have given ourselves over so completely to selfishness that we hurt not only those around us but ourselves even more deeply and casually that one must assume a blunting of the imagination and sense of danger of truly psychiatric proportions.

Rampaging selfishness is another name for indiscipline, and its prime objective is to free the self from a constraining sense of another and of fair-play. Mr B sees Mr A ahead of him in the queue or in the traffic. He does not reason that Mr A is there because he took the trouble to arrive early. He says instead: *he is where I want to be; he must give way to me.* In the scuffle that follows, someone will get hurt. Even the prize for which the queue was originally mounted may get smashed in the fray. But these are already remote, unfamiliar considerations. The prize *now* is the action.

I will now direct our attention to a species of indiscipline which by its very nature is much more dangerous than the indiscipline of taxi-drivers and such like. I refer to the indiscipline of leaders and people in authority.

Leaders are, in the language of psychologists, role models. People look up to them and copy their actions, behaviour and even mannerisms. Therefore if a leader lacks discipline the effect is apt to spread automatically down to his followers. The less discerning among these (i.e. the vast majority) will accept his action quite simply as 'the done thing,' while the more critical may worry about it for a while and then settle the matter by telling themselves that the normal rules of social behaviour need not apply to those in power.

Either way something noxious has been released into the very air the people breathe – an emanation stronger than precedent; stronger because its association with power gives it a strange potential to fascinate the powerless.

Those with a strong appetite for power understand this phenomenon very well and go out of their way to cultivate the mystique of power, even of ruthless power. The NPP slogan *Power to the People!* conveniently abbreviated to *Power!* proved brilliant and effective in Anambra and Imo in 1979 and was publicized by the most powerless element in society: the children. Seeing the result the NPN, like a second-rate copy-writer, came up with *Super Power!* for 1983. Fortunately for society power does not only entice, intimidate and subdue; it may also incite to resentment and rebellion.

Manifestations of this mood may look very much like indiscipline. Indeed it will be so called by authority and its protagonists. But what about us? Let us examine a simple, and quite common, example: Students in a boarding school go on the rampage, burning and smashing things including the Principal's car. Our automatic reaction is to scream: Indiscipline!, make a few woolly and pessimistic statements about this country and perhaps offer the standard evasive prescription – to hand schools over to religious bodies! (Just as parents unable to cope had handed their children over to schools in the first place!) We have now become a *handing-over* nation. But be that as it may. Now supposing on closer examination of the school incident we should discover that the children's complaint about bad food is legitimate, that the Principal has been pilfering their food money to build himself a house in his village, shall we still call their action indiscipline? No doubt the Principal will. But the rest of us are not obliged to.

In summary the indiscipline of an ordinary citizen, regrettable as it may be, does not pose a fatal threat to society because it can be generally contained by his fellows or, at worst, by a couple of policemen. But the indiscipline of a leader is a different matter altogether. First, he has no fellows to restrain him, and the policemen who might have done it are all in his employ. Second, *power*, by giving him immunity from common censure, makes the leader the envy of the powerless who will turn him into a role model and imitate his actions of indiscipline. An explosion of such actions occurring all over the place at once brings the whole society under a *climate of indiscipline*. Third, and fortunately, a leader's undisciplined actions can also incite to anger and rebellion.

It is not my purpose here to argue whether or not anger and rebellion are justified in these circumstances. They are! I only suggest that these eruptions having no selfish motivation cannot constitute indiscipline. At worst they are the price, sometimes exceedingly heavy, which society pays for the luxury of having a bad leader.

I will conclude this chapter with actual descriptions of indiscipline by leaders to illustrate what I have been saying.

Three years ago I was foolish enough to be on the Enugu-Onitsha road on December 23. At the Abagana-Otuocha junction my slow and perilous progress was finally finished, by the look of things, for the year. We had descended into pandemonium.

But a miracle happened after more than two hours. A band of koboko-wielding policemen arrived on the scene from nowhere and went furiously to work on the drivers who had left their traffic lane. For the first time in my life I found myself loudly cheering the savage administration of corporal punishment as I saw the road clearing with miraculous speed towards my place of confinement. And then something quite extraordinary happened before my eyes. A mobile policeman raised his whip and then lowered it, transferred it quickly to his left hand and saluted.

Then I saw. Beside the driver he had been about to whip sat a police orderly. In the back, through lightly tinted glass, I saw a Judge.

The mobile policeman now had a new task (which he performed with equal zeal) of seeing His Lordship out of a tight corner and on his way before he resumed, with visibly less energy, his original assignment. Fortunately, enough work had already been accomplished before the judicial interruption and traffic flow was soon restored and we were all able to get home for Christmas.

I realized a few days later what an unfailing touch

Shakespeare had had. In his *Julius Caesar* he had observed that very sight in the closest detail four hundred years before I stumbled on it at the Abagana junction:

> The name of Cassius honours this corruption
> And chastisement doth therefore hide his head

(For *Cassius* read *His Lordship*)

Unlucky is the country where indiscipline is seen by ordinary people as the prerogative of the high and mighty. For, by the same token, discipline will be seen as a penalty which the rank and file must pay for their powerlessness. The consequences of such a view on the mental attitudes of a people are too glaring for words. But that is precisely the view which Nigerian elite groups foster in their private and public behaviour. The queue is for the little man; the big man has no use for it. Observe the boarding of Nigerian planes, how the VIPs in their suits or feathers walk up to the gangway absolutely oblivious of the waiting line of ordinary travellers. I don't know any other country where you can find such brazen insensitivity and arrogant selfishness among those who lay claim to leadership and education, or where the ordinary people put up with such arrant nonsense.

And why, in any case does the Nigeria Airways find it impossible to run even a moderately civilized service with seat allocation on boarding passes? Is such elementary competence really beyond us?

I must now touch, however briefly, on the grave undermining of national discipline which the *siren mentality* of Nigerian leaders fosters.

In all civilized countries the siren is used in grave emergencies by fire engines, ambulances and the police in actual pursuit of crime. Nigeria, with its remarkable genius for travesty, has found a way to turn yet another useful invention by serious-minded people elsewhere into a childish and cacophonous instrument for the celebration of status.

In other places the movement of presidents and governors is a sober, business-like affair. In Nigeria it is a medieval chieftain's progress complete with magicians and wild acrobats chasing citizens out of the way. Has it never occurred to anybody that the brutal aggressiveness which precedes a leader's train leaves a more lasting impression on the national psychology than the hollow, after-thought smile and hand-waving two minutes later? Is there no one in this country perceptive enough to understand that after two decades of bloodshed and military rule what our society craves today is not a style of leadership which projects and celebrates the violence of power but the sobriety of peace?

Last year I was a guest of the Irish Government at the centenary of James Joyce. I sat with other guests and thousands of Dubliners in a huge municipal hall waiting for the President of the Irish Republic to arrive and inaugurate the event. Two minutes to go and I had still not seen any signs of his arrival. On the exact dot of five a tall fellow walked on to the stage followed by *one* man in uniform. The Chairman of the event (who incidentally was a writer and not the Irish Minister for Social Affairs, Sports, Children, Women, Trade Unions and Culture) motioned the audience to stand. So that was the President! His ADC gave him his speech which he read and came down to sit in the audience to listen to a few tributes to Joyce.

The argument of Security which is always raised by defenders of official thuggery surrounding executive appearances in Nigeria has never been persuasive. Security is hindered, not enhanced, in a climate of hooliganism.

But I am prepared to leave matters of security to those who claim expertise in the matter. I will only remind them and those who heed their advice that there are more political assassinations in mentally under-developed countries which indulge in the celebration and brandishing of Power than in mature countries which sublimate it. But as our people might say: wetin be my concern there?

What should and does concern all of us is the danger of indiscipline by imitation which I have already referred to *ad nauseam* but must return to one last time in the form of an actual incident.

Early in 1983 I was travelling from Nsukka to Ogidi with my wife and daughter and driver. As we were driving through Awka we heard a siren and performed the appropriate motions of mild panic and pulled up. Three police vehicles – a jeep, a car and a lorry – sped by in the opposite direction. From the side of the lorry a policeman was pissing on to the road and the halted traffic.

You may not believe it; and I can't say I blame you. Although I clearly saw the fly of his trousers, his sprinkler and the jet of urine, I still would not have believed it if

I had not had confirmation in the horrified reaction of other travellers around us, and if my wife and driver had not recoiled instinctively from the impact of that police piss on their side of the car. Fortunately for them the glass was wound up.

It was almost humorous.

Postscript

The wanton and colossal destruction of national resources – life and limb, public utilities and private property – on our highways is a thousand times more grievous than the wildest threat armed robbers and other violent criminals can pose to our society's security.

In non-material terms mass indiscipline on the road, which has long deteriorated into lawlessness, fosters a national *style* which must and does inevitably spill over into other areas of national conduct.

We must now recognize the emergency status of this situation and treat it accordingly. The descent into 'mere anarchy' must be halted and reversed.

A Presidential Commission on Road Safety is urgently called for. It should be given sweeping powers to draw up and implement a programme for sanity on Nigerian roads. This is not another Commission for Emirs and religious leaders to sit on or an opportunity to reward party stalwarts. A serious and business-like Commission will not only tackle and solve the problem at hand, it will also remove the excuse of certain state governments for creating para-military formations for political purposes.

8 Corruption

Quite recently an astonishing statement credited to President Shagari was given some publicity in Nigeria and abroad. According to the media our President said words to the effect that there was corruption in Nigeria but that it had not yet reached alarming proportions.

My frank and honest opinion is that anybody who can say that corruption in Nigeria has not yet become alarming is either a fool, a crook or else does not live in this country.

Shagari is neither a fool nor a crook. So I must assume that he lives abroad. Which is not as strange or fanciful as some might think. Many Presidents, especially Third World Presidents, do not live in their country. One of the penalties of exalted power is loneliness. Harnessed to the trappings of protocol and blockaded by a buffer of grinning courtiers and sycophants, even a good and intelligent leader will gradually begin to forget what the real world looks like.

When a President of Nigeria sets out to see things for himself, what does he actually see?

Highways temporarily cleared of lunatic drivers by even more lunatic presidential escorts; hitherto impassable tracks freshly graded and even watered to keep down the dust; buildings dripping fresh paint; well-fed obsequious welcoming parties; garlands of colourful toilet paper hung round the neck by women leaders; troupes of 'cultural dancers' in the sun, and many other such scenes of contented citizenry. But history tells us of wise rulers at different times and places who achieved rare leadership by their blunt and simple refusal to be fooled by guided tours of their own country. In antiquity we read, for example, of Haroun al Rashid, an eighth-century caliph of Baghdad, who frequently disguised himself and went unaccompanied into the streets of his city by day or night to see the life of his subjects in its ungarnished and uncensored reality. Modern history has its examples too, but they may be too close for comfort.

So Shehu Shagari should return home, read the papers and from time to time talk to Nigerians outside the circle of Presidential aides and party faithfuls.

Corruption in Nigeria has *passed* the alarming and *entered* the fatal stage; and Nigeria will die if we keep pretending that she is only slightly indisposed.

The *Weekly Star* of 15 May 1983 has this on its front page under the title *The Nigerian and Corruption*:

> Keeping an average Nigerian from being corrupt is like keeping a goat from eating yam.

This is a bad way of putting it, worse perhaps than the President's denial of its severity. A goat needs yam because yam is food for goats. A Nigerian does not need corruption, neither is corruption necessary nourishment for Nigerians. It is totally false to suggest, as we are apt to do, that Nigerians are different fundamentally from any other people in the world. Nigerians are corrupt because the system under which they live today makes corruption easy and profitable; they will cease to be corrupt when corruption is made difficult and inconvenient.

Furthermore the concept of 'the average Nigerian' in this connection is hardly helpful. If indeed there is such a creature as 'an average Nigerian' he is likely to be found at a point in social space with limited opportunities for corruption as we generally understand the word. Corruption goes with power; and whatever the average man may have it is *not* power. Therefore to hold any useful discussion of corruption we must first locate it where it properly belongs – in the ranks of the powerful.

The ostrich evasion of President Shagari and the fatalistic acceptance of the *Weekly Star* writer are among the major obstacles to a proper assessment of, and solution to, the problem of rampant corruption in Nigeria.

As I write this in my hotel room in Kano (Monday 16 May 1983) I have two of this morning's papers on my table – *National Concord* and *Daily Times*. I shall go no further for my examples of Nigerian corruption.

The *Concord* carries a banner headline: FRAUD AT P and T, followed by a story with no less authority than that of the Federal Minister of Communications, Mr Audu Ogbe, that 'the Federal Government is losing ₦50 million every month as salaries' to non-existent workers.

In the course of one year then Nigeria loses ₦600 million in this particular racket. A series of little comparisons may bring home the size of this loss.

With ₦600 million Nigeria could build two more international airports like the Murtala Muhammed Airport in Lagos; or if we are not keen on more airports the money could buy us three refineries; or build us a dual express motorway from Lagos to Kaduna; or pay the salary of 10,000 workers on grade level 01 for forty years!

And please remember that Minister Audu Ogbe is not telling us about *all* the fraud in the Posts and Telegraphs Department but only about *one* particular racket which has just come to light: payment of salaries to fictitious workers.

And please, please remember also that Mr Audu Ogbe is in no position to inform us about fraud in other Federal parastatals; not to talk of state government companies and corporations; not to talk of the Federal Civil Service including, if you please, the Department of Customs and Excise; not to talk of nineteen state civil services; not to talk of Local Governments, or Abuja, or etc., etc., etc. And of course there is the completely different world of the Private Sector!

Would it be too fanciful then to reckon that the sum of all the fraud committed against the people of Nigeria in the public and the private services would come to a figure so staggering as completely to boggle the imagination?

We have become so used to talking in millions and billions that we have ceased to have proper respect for the sheer size of such numbers. I sometimes startled my students by telling them that it was not yet one million *days* since Christ was on earth. As they gazed open-mouthed I would add: Not even half-a-million days!

In traditional Igbo lore numbers like one million are called *agukata agba awari*: you count and count till your jaw breaks. And yet it is now the prime ambition of so many to steal so much from the nation.

Now let's look at the other paper on my table. The *Daily Times* editorial headlined *The Fake Importers* brings us another revelation, this time at the ports – a story of Nigerian importers who having applied for and obtained scarce foreign exchange from the Central Bank ostensibly to pay for raw materials overseas, leave the money in their banks abroad and ship to Lagos containers of mud and sand!

I consider myself a reasonably humane person, but I must confess that after reading that editorial I dredged up from the depths of my psyche the following punishment: insert the importer head-first into his mud, seal the container once more and ship it back to his overseas collaborators!

These two stories – the payment of ghost workers at the Posts and Telegraphs and the importation of mud into Nigeria – are carried by two newspapers which I just happen to have bought this morning. If I had more papers or more days to choose from I could multiply such scandals and frauds against the nation a hundred-fold, nay, a thousand!

Knowledgeable observers have estimated that as much as 60 per cent of the wealth of this nation is regularly consumed by corruption. I have no doubt that defenders of our system would retort: Mere rumours! Where is the proof?

No one can offer 'satisfactory' proof for the simple reason that nobody issues a receipt for a bribe or for money stolen from the public till. We do know, however, that when the revolution which such scandalous behaviour invites does come, proofs tend all of a sudden to pour out in torrential abundance. Meanwhile, as thieves say to one another, mum's the word!

So we must fall back on intelligent observation, surmises, estimations and even rumours.

A few years ago a new cultural facility was opened in London by Queen Elizabeth II. It was called the Barbican Centre and it cost the British tax-payer £150 million, which is roughly equivalent to ₦180 million. It was such a magnificent structure that one account described it as the Eighth Wonder of the World.

We know that Nigeria in the last decade has built many structures worth more (or rather that *cost* more) than ₦180 million. But show me one wonder among them, unless it be the wonder of discrepancy between cost and value!

The reason for this is quite simple. A structure that costs us, say ₦200 million carries a huge hidden element of kick-backs and commissions to Nigerian middlemen and, increasingly, middlewomen; it carries inflated prices of materials caused largely by corruption; theft and inefficiency on the site fostered by more corruption; contract variations corruptly arranged midstream in execution, an inflated margin (or, more aptly, corridor) of profit. When all these factors are added to others which our corrupt ingenuity constantly invents, you will be lucky if on completion (assuming such a happy event occurs) your structure is worth as much as ₦80 million.

It would be impossible and, even if possible, of little value to attempt a comprehensive picture of the types and scope of Nigerian corruption. I will only say that most people will agree that corruption has grown enormously in variety, magnitude and brazenness since the beginning of the Second Republic because it has been extravagantly fuelled by budgetary abuse and political patronage on an unprecedented scale.

Public funds are now routinely doled out to political allies and personal friends in the guise of contracts to execute public works of one kind or another, or licences to import restricted commodities. Generally a political contractor will have no expertise whatsoever nor even the intention to perform. He will simply sell the contract to a third party and pocket the commission running into hundreds of thousands of naira or even millions for acting as a conduit of executive fiat.

Alternatively he can raise cash not by selling the contract but by collecting a 'mobilization fee' from the Treasury, putting aside the contract for the time being or for ever, buying himself a Mercedes Benz car and seeking elective office through open and massive bribery.

If in spite of all his exertions he still fails to win nomination or is defeated at the polls he may be rewarded with a ministerial appointment. Should he as minister find himself engulfed in serious financial scandal the President will promptly re-assign him – to another ministry.

Although Nigeria is without any shadow of doubt one of the most corrupt nations in the world there has not been one high public officer in the twenty-three years of our independence who has been made to face the music for official corruption. And so, from fairly timid manifestations in the 1960s, corruption has grown bold and ravenous as, with each succeeding regime, our public servants have become more reckless and blatant.

As we have sunk more and more deeply into the

quagmire we have been 'blessed' with a succession of leaders who are said to possess impeccable personal integrity but unfortunately are surrounded by sharks and crooks. I do confess to some personal difficulty in even beginning to visualize genuine integrity in that kind of fix; for it has always seemed to me that the test of integrity is its blunt refusal to be compromised.

But be that as it may, we are all living witnesses to the failure of helpless integrity to solve the problem of rampant corruption which threatens now to paralyse this country in every sinew and every limb.

Obviously this situation which has built up over the years will take some time to correct, assuming we want to do it peacefully. But to initiate change the President of this country must take, and be seen to take, a decisive first step of ridding his administration of all persons on whom the slightest wind of corruption and scandal has blown. When he can summon up the courage to do that he will find himself grown overnight to such stature and authority that he will become Nigeria's leader, not just its president. Only then can he take on and conquer corruption in the nation.

9 The Igbo Problem

A distinguished political scientist from a 'minority' area of the south pronounced some years ago that *Nigeria has an Igbo problem*. Every ethnic group is of course something of a problem for Nigeria's easy achievement of cohesive nationhood. But the learned professor no doubt saw the Igbo as a particular irritant, a special thorn in the flesh of the Nigerian body-politic.

Nigerians of all other ethnic groups will probably achieve consensus on no other matter than their common resentment of the Igbo. They would all describe them as *aggressive*, *arrogant* and *clannish*. Most would add *grasping* and *greedy* (although the performance of the Yoruba since the end of the Civil War has tended to put the prize for greed in some doubt!).

Modern Nigerian history has been marked by sporadic eruptions of anti-Igbo feeling of more or less serious import; but it was not until 1966–7 when it swept through Northern Nigeria like 'a flood of deadly hate' that the Igbo first questioned the concept of Nigeria which they had embraced with much greater fervour than the Yoruba or the Hausa/Fulani.

The Civil War gave Nigeria a perfect and legitimate excuse to cast the Igbo in the role of treasonable felon, a wrecker of the nation. But thanks to Gowon's moderating influence overt vengeance was not visited on them when their secessionist State of Biafra was defeated in January 1970. But there were hard-liners in Gowon's cabinet who wanted their pound of flesh, the most powerful among them being Chief Obafemi Awolowo, Federal Commissioner for Finance. Under his guidance a banking policy was evolved which nullified any bank account which had been operated during the Civil War. This had the immediate result of pauperizing the Igbo middle class and earning a profit of £4 million for the Federal Government Treasury.

The Indigenization Decree which followed soon

afterwards completed the routing of the Igbo from the commanding heights of the Nigerian economy, to everyone's apparent satisfaction.

The origin of the national resentment of the Igbo is as old as Nigeria and quite as complicated. But it can be summarized thus: The Igbo culture being receptive to change, individualistic and highly competitive, gave the Igbo man an unquestioned advantage over his compatriots in securing credentials for advancement in Nigerian colonial society. Unlike the Hausa/Fulani he was unhindered by a wary religion and unlike the Yoruba unhampered by traditional hierarchies. This kind of creature, fearing nor God nor man, was custom-made to grasp the opportunities, such as they were, of the white man's dispensation. And the Igbo did so with both hands. Although the Yoruba had a huge historical and geographical head-start the Igbo wiped out their handicap in one fantastic burst of energy in the twenty years between 1930 and 1950.

Had the Igbo been a minor ethnic group of a few hundred thousand, their menace might have been easily and quietly contained. But they ran in their millions! Like J.P. Clark's fine image of 'ants filing out of the wood' the Igbo moved out of their forest home, scattered and virtually seized the floor.

But this kind of success can carry a deadly penalty: the danger of *hubris*, over-weening pride and thoughtlessness, which invites envy and hatred; or even worse, which can obsess the mind with material success and dispose it to all kinds of crude showiness.

There is no doubt at all that there is a strand in contemporary Igbo behaviour which can offend by its noisy exhibitionism and disregard for humility and quietness. If you walk into the crowded waiting-room at the Ikeja Airport on one of those days when all flights are delayed or cancelled 'for operational reasons' and you hear one man's voice high over a subdued and despondent multitude the chances are he will be an Igbo man who 'has made it' and is desperate to be noticed and admired.

The other charge which is levelled against the Igbo is clannishness. He is accused of unduly favouring his kindred and running to their defence at all times. He is supposed to have a tribal caucus where decisions are made and conspiracies hatched to advance Igbo interests.

Such pan-Igbo solidarity is a figment of the Nigerian imagination. It has never existed except briefly, and for a unique reason, during the Civil War.

The rise of the Igbo in Nigerian affairs was due to the self-confidence engendered by their open society and their belief that one man is as good as another, that no condition is permanent. It was not due, as non-Igbo observers have imagined, to tribal mutual aid societies. The 'Town Union' phenomenon which has often been written about was in reality an extension of the Igbo individualistic ethic. The Igbo towns competed among themselves for certain kinds of social achievement, like building of schools, churches, markets, post offices, pipe-borne water projects, roads, etc. They did not concern themselves with pan-Igbo unity nor were they geared to securing an advantage over non-Igbo Nigerians. Beyond town or village the Igbo has no compelling traditional loyalty.

The Igbo State Union was a paper tiger whose bogey value may have been exploited by a handful of self-appointed leaders in such places as Lagos and Port Harcourt; but among the Igbo elite it was largely a joke and to the Igbo masses it was quite unknown.

The real problem with the Igbo since Independence is precisely the absence of the kind of central leadership which their competitors presume for them. This lack has left them open to self-seeking, opportunistic, leaders who offered them no help at all in coping with a new Nigeria in which individual progress would no longer depend on the rules set by a fairly impartial colonial umpire.

The lack of real leaders in Igboland goes back, of course, to the beginnings of colonial administration. Once the white man had crushed Igbo resistance it was relatively easy for him to locate upstarts and ruffians in the community who would uphold his regime at the expense of their own people. From those days the average Igbo leader's mentality has not been entirely free of the collaborating Warrant Chief syndrome.

The bankrupt state of Igbo leadership is best illustrated in the alacrity with which they have jettisoned their traditional republicanism in favour of mushroom kingships. From having no kings in their recent past the Igbo swung round to set an all-time record of four hundred 'kings' in Imo and four hundred in Anambra! And most of them are traders in their stall by day and monarchs at night; city dwellers five days a week and traditional village rulers on Saturdays and Sundays! They adopt 'traditional' robes from every land, including,

I am told, the ceremonial regalia of the Lord Mayor of London!

The degree of travesty to which the Igbo man is apparently ready to reduce his institutions in his eagerness 'to get up' can be truly amazing. At first sight this weakness might appear only as a private problem for the Igbo themselves. But an indifference to non-material values which it portrays might easily spill over into a carelessness and a disregard for the feelings of sacredness which others might hold for their own institutions. And there is a great danger of social friction in this. So it becomes necessary that while Nigeria is at the delicate, touch-and-go stage of national evolution, the Igbo must learn less abrasiveness, more shrewdness and tact and a willingness to grant the validity of less boisterous values.

Having said all that, there is no doubt in my mind that the competitive individualism and the adventurous spirit of the Igbo are necessary ingredients in the modernization and development of Nigerian society. It is neither necessary, nor indeed possible, to suppress them. Nigeria without the inventiveness and the dynamism of the Igbo would be a less hopeful place than it is.

The policy of overt and covert exclusion and discrimination beginning with Awolowo's banking regulations at the end of the Civil War and pursued relentlessly by the Muhammed/Obasanjo administration has had its day and must now end in the interest of stability and progress.

In a famous motion which was disallowed for mysterious reasons by the President of the Nigerian Senate and subsequently published by its author after resigning his

Senate seat, Mr F. J. Ellah has drawn attention to what can only be called the Muhammed-Obasanjo conspiracy by which four states and a considerable interest in a fifth were given to the Yoruba while their Igbo competitors of about equal population got two. This was done in preparation for a new fiscal arrangement in which states would determine what share of Federal allocations went to whom. The gross inequity here must be apparent to anyone who is not blinded by prejudice or self-interest.

Arguments about siting major Federal industries, huge irrigation schemes and agricultural projects of revolutionary dimensions may seem tiresome to Federal Ministers visiting Anambra and Imo States and having to explain away so much in television interviews. But there is no way in which any one with the slightest interest in fairness can begin to excuse the transparent discrimination of past and present Federal governments in this regard.

Many have tried but nobody has quite succeeded in explaining away the siting of five steel mills worth ₦4.5 billion on final completion, with estimated employment capacity of 100,000 by 1990, only in the North and West of the country.

The hypocrisy and guilt attendant upon such a gigantic abuse of elementary fair-play was 'beautifully' demonstrated in a November 9, 1982 *National Concord* report: 'Wonders of Katsina Steel Mill,' by one Ola Amupitan. Here is part of his report:

> No question was considered too preposterous for the Minister. He was called upon to explain why the spread

of mills left out the eastern south of Nigeria. Malam Ali Makele said it was not fair to reach such a dangerous conclusion. He said there was a mill affiliated to Aladja meant to sell steel products to Bendel, Cross River, Rivers, Imo and Anambra States.

Why, you may ask, does journalist Amupitan consider a simple question *preposterous*? Why does Ali Makele consider it *unfair* and even *dangerous*? It is because their case is hopelessly weak and they know that the verdict can be nothing other than *guilty*. It is not the question which is preposterous, unfair and dangerous, but the siting of steel mills. And they know it. And Nigeria knows it.

That is why these two – Amupitan and Makele – are attempting so strenuously and so vainly the forensic somersault of transferring guilt from a crime to its mere observation. That is why they are using threatening language to blackmail and intimidate the observer into silence.

When Nigeria learns to deal fairly with all its citizens (including the troublesome Igbo) the defenders of its policies will have an easier time in court than Amupitan and Makele had on this one. And its prospects for progress and stability will be infinitely brighter.

10 The Example of Aminu Kano

This final chapter was prompted, quite understandably I hope, by the recent death of Mallam Aminu Kano. But I do not intend to make it a tribute in the traditional mode, but rather to use it in the manner of Aminu Kano himself to ask the crucial question: What is the purpose of political power?

Anyone who saw Aminu Kano's last television interview will recall that he insisted, with an urgency most moving in retrospect, on that primary question: Why do you seek political office? Why do you want to rule?

We know, of course, that every politician gives us an answer to that question. Unfortunately their answers are so alike as to leave us totally unenlightened.

On my return after a recent trip outside Anambra State I was accosted at the Enugu Airport by a stranger who turned out to be Alhaji Onyeama, a leading Igbo moslem. He was puzzled, he told me, by all the praise that politicans were heaping on Aminu Kano since he died. If they thought so highly of him, why did they not join his party?

A naive question? Not at all!

Some days later, on NTA news the Anglican Bishop on the Niger, the Right Reverend Jonathan Onyemelukwe, was appealing to politicians to spare us violence and threats of violence at this year's elections. After all, he said, you have told us that you want our votes so that you can serve us. If we get killed while you are getting the vote, who then will you serve?

Another naive question? Far from it! Bishop Onyemelukwe is a highly sophisticated and intellectual churchman.

Behind these two questions – Alhaji Onyeama's and the bishop's – lie a deep scepticism about the politician's professed motives and, flowing from that doubt, a call to wariness on the part of the victim.

For we are victims. The entire Nigerian populace constitutes one huge, helpless electoral dupe in the hands of the politician / victimizer. We know, of course, that politicians everywhere will attempt to deceive and hoodwink. But there must be very few places in the world outside one-party states where they succeed as admirably as they do in this country.

The Chinese have a very wise proverb: fool me once, shame on you; fool me again, shame on me!

The Nigerian electorate by now should have sunk deep into the ground under the sheer weight of its electoral shame; for it has allowed itself to be fooled not twice but twice-two-hundred times!

Why is this so? Are Nigerians more stupid than other people? No, we are not. But as in every other department of our national life we perform below our potential, like a car with a little water in its fuel tank, accumulated dirt in its carburettor and carbon deposit on its spark plugs. In the specific matter of elections we have deprived ourselves of our potential power over politicians by falling prey to ethnicity and other divisive bogeys they conjure up and harness to their band-waggon.

While the electorate is thus emasculated by such instigated divisions, the successful politician will link up even with his tribal enemy once they get to the legislature in order to promote measures of common interest to their new elite class. Witness the marvellous cooperation with which our National Assembly took over accommodation provided for civil servants on Victoria Island; how quickly they pass bills to increase their emoluments, unite to cover up members' wrongdoing, or devise a national order of precedence in which they feature prominently, without recourse to the electorate! (It should be pointed out that in this matter of a National Order of Precedence which was surprisingly – but characteristically – of such importance to our legislators, it was left to an outsider, Dr J. O. J. Okezie, to point out that university Vice-Chancellors were not even mentioned.)

Therefore the ethnic and other divisions which the politician inflicts so assiduously on the nation in his periodic pursuit of electoral goals do not benefit the voter in any way. On the contrary, they deprive him of the power to hold the politician truly accountable through common action with other voters across the land. In effect the Nigerian voter is effectively disenfranchised by these divisions.

Therefore he must wake up to this danger. He must now begin to ask the crucial question: why do you want my vote? And he must treat the easy answer of the politician with appropriate scepticism.

These are by no means easy habits to cultivate, especially where the masses of the population have so little access to untainted information. But arduous as the task is, Nigeria's educated elite must understand that they have no choice but to address themselves to it or receive history's merciless indictment. All those enlightened and thoughtful Nigerians who wring their hands in daily anguish on account of our wretched performance as a nation must bestir themselves to the patriotic action of proselytizing for decent and civilized political values. We have stood too long on the side-lines; and too many of us have adopted the cynical attitude that since you cannot beat them you must join them.

Our inaction or cynical action are a serious betrayal of our education, of our historic mission and of succeeding generations who will have no future unless we save it *now* for them. To be educated is, after all, to develop the questioning habit, to be sceptical of easy promises and to use past experience creatively.

In 1979 we deluded ourselves in the belief that we were politically more sophisticated than we had been in the First Republic. We told ourselves that a new generation of voters had come of age who had not been born under colonialism. We were certain that a generation that had suffered so much bloodshed and war would not tolerate the kind of politics and politicians whose excesses had unleashed that Armageddon on a defenceless people while taking care that the guilty went completely unscathed. We looked around and saw all the new universities and colleges of technology and a formidable army of new graduates who did not suffer the poverty complex of their self-made fathers and would therefore not grasp at every kobo in sight, and we nodded in satisfaction. And to cap it all, we assumed that a nation which had seen thirteen years of military dictatorship and its abysmal failure to correct the political and social abuses it had promised to set right, would guard most jealously its newly restored democratic processes.

But we were wrong on every score. The politics of the Second Republic has demonstrated the Shavian conceit that the only thing we learn from experience is that we learn nothing from experience.

We have turned out to be like a bunch of stage clowns who bump their heads into the same heavy obstacles again and again because they are too stupid to remember what hit them only a short while ago. The reason for this strange forgetfulness was the return to our national stage and in full combatant vigour of two of the three political gladiators of the First Republic: Dr Nnamdi Azikiwe and Chief Obafemi Awolowo. This return was an unmitigated disaster.

I did not share the view which was canvassed in some quarters that these venerable gentleman should have been banned from partisan politics. Bans are always an admission of failure. And in any case, since our Constitution (quite sensibly) did not prescribe an upper age limit for political activity it is difficult to see on what grounds such an unjust prohibition could be based. What one had hoped was that an enlightened electorate such as we had presumed had come into being, would have listened politely to what these two had to say and sent them quietly home again.

But that was not to be. The 'new breed' of politicians – young, aggressive, impatient for power, impatient of slow slogging – saw two alternatives and promptly settled for the one that promised immediate gratification. The first alternative was to build a new political consciousness out of our recent tragic experience and the universal desire for a new social order. The second alternative was to use the name and remnant mystique of the old masters and then, if need be . . .

So the young ambitious politicians went to work among the Igbo and the Yoruba dusting up the reputation of their old magicians, re-writing history here and there to suit the circumstances of 1979.

The task before the up-and-coming Yoruba politicians was by far easier than what their Igbo counterparts had to accomplish. Awolowo had been a steadfast Yoruba nationalist from the 1940s to date. He had no record of betrayal, double-talk or even indecision in the pursuit of his goals. But above all he had in recent years as the leading civilian member of the Gowon administration presided over a monumental transfer and consolidation of economic, bureaucratic and professional power to his home base.

This singular achievement secured for Awolowo for the first time in his political career something approaching 100 per cent support among the Yoruba.

So the task before the 'new breed' Yoruba politicians was not to convince their home audience for they were already well convinced. Perhaps all that was needed was to anchor their conviction on mysticism. And so we witnessed the bizarre situation in which serious newspapers in Yorubaland carried stories of miracles wrought by Papa Awolowo.

But unfortunately for them (and fortunately for Nigeria, I think) they had to convince non-Yoruba Nigerians as well. And there they found their product pretty unmarketable. Not that it stopped them from trying!

The saddest aspect of their endeavour, in my view, was the mental gymnastic of my academic and professional colleagues. Capitalists among them avoided ideology and concentrated on Papa's record of administrative efficiency. One such campaigner, imagining my sympathies, told me that Papa was the only Southern Nigerian politician who had consistently stood up against the

North. I told him that when the Igbo did precisely that they did not recall hearing very much from Papa.

But it was the Yoruba radical and socialist who cut the most interesting figure during his *agit-prop* among erstwhile ideological colleagues. It did not seem to bother him that in no known tradition of socialist thought (not even in the permissive sub-species known as African Socialism) can you be allowed to pass off millionaire land-grabbers as promising material for social reconstruction.

The NPP politicians had a different kind of problem because of Azikiwe's consistent ambivalence to his ethnic homeland. The eager young politician who needed desperately to latch on to Azikiwe's huge but heavily tarnished prestige had first to re-write large chunks of recent Nigerian history (and is in fact doing it still) to explain away Azikiwe's abandonment of Igbo people in their darkest hour.

Some observers have wondered why Dr Azikiwe who had been everything Nigeria could offer – first Premier of Eastern Nigeria, first Nigerian President of the Senate, first Nigerian Governor-General, first President – should suddenly abandon his dignified retirement and return once more to the hustings with certainty of electoral defeat in 1979.

I suspect that Zik, among whose faults is not political naivety, was engaged primarily in a battle for a rehabilitation of his place in Igbo history and only marginally for the Nigerian presidency. Unlike many of the brash and not very intelligent young politicians who clamoured around his giant figure and climbed to power on his back,

Azikiwe has a fair sense of the inexorable power of history's judgement of people and events, and was prepared to gamble with electoral defeat if in the process he might be offered a chance to alter the records in his favour in one or two unflattering pages of recent history.

To be able to do this he realized he needed the apparatus of government which the Asika administration had failed to make available to him earlier. So Azikiwe seized the new opportunity and threw in his lot with the eager young men who had come to use him. He would help them to gain state power, and then use them to inaugurate a massive propaganda effort to redeem his reputation.

Three key factors helped this symbiotic arrangement to achieve its objectives in Imo and Anambra States. First and foremost is the inclination of the Igbo to jettison his traditions (including his history) if he sees personal advancement accruing from such abandonment. A sufficient number of 'new-breed' politicians saw precisely such a prospect for themselves in the nebulous indeterminacy of 1979, and seized it. Few of them had any illusions about Azikiwe's credentials. I remember one of them quoting one of the most blatantly opportunistic Igbo proverbs in support of what he was doing: if you see an udala fruit beside a mound of shit, pluck a leaf and cover the shit and take your fruit!

The second factor was the Nigerian politician's inevitable stand-by and resort – playing on the tribal chord. Dr Azikiwe was the only Igbo among the five presidential candidates. His temporary tax problem with Fedeco was alleged to be deliberately instigated. What more was there to say?

The recourse to ethnicity was aided by a third factor which was closely related to it – the intrinsic weakness of appeal in Igboland of Azikiwe's major competitors: Obafemi Awolowo and Shehu Shagari. Chief Awolowo had a well-deserved reputation for anti-Igbo politics which, over a period of years, had permeated every stratum of Igbo society. And although Shagari did not inspire similar personal antipathy he did inherit the odium of the 1966 massacres in the North and the later Federal Government discrimination against Igbo areas during the military administration in which he, even more than Awolowo, had participated.

It was not surprising, therefore, that although many Igbo entertained serious reservations about Azikiwe and his band of unknown aspirants in 1979 they allowed themselves to be conned into believing that there was no other fruit but this one to pick. So they blotted out the unwholesome background with leaves; and ate it.

But the problem with Azikiwe's political career in Nigeria or even his relationship with the Igbo has never been how to explain away one momentary lapse in an otherwise steady record of standing fast but rather how to account for a pretty consistent history of abandonments.

Here was an eloquent revolutionary who inspired a whole generation of young idealistic activists in the Zikist Movement to the high pitch of positive action against colonial rule and then, quite unaccountably, abandoned them at the prison gate.

Here was a true nationalist who championed the noble cause of 'one Nigeria' to the extent that he contested and won the first general election to the Western House of Assembly. But when Chief Awolowo 'stole' the government from him in broad daylight he abandoned his principle which dictated that he should stay in the Western House as Leader of the Opposition and give battle to Awolowo. Instead he conceded victory to reactionary ethnic politics, fled to the East where he compounded his betrayal of principle by precipitating a major crisis which was unnecessary, selfish and severely damaging in its consequences.

Professor Eyo Ita, an urbane and detribalized humanist politician who had just assumed office as Leader of Government Business in Enugu, saw no reason to vacate his post for the fugitive from Ibadan. Neither did most of his cabinet which in sheer brilliance surpassed by far anything Enugu has seen or is likely to see again in a long time.

Using his privately owned newspapers and political muscle Azikiwe maligned and forced Eyo Ita and his team out of office and proceeded to pack his own cabinet with primary school teachers, ex-police corporals, sanitary inspectors and similar highly motivated disciples who were unlikely to dispute anything he said. So the rule of mediocrity from which we suffer today received an early *imprimatur* in Eastern Nigeria, of all places!

And that was not all. Professor Eyo Ita was an Efik, and the brutally unfair treatment offered him in Enugu did not go unremarked in Calabar. It contributed in no small measure to the suspicion of the majority Igbo by their minority neighbours in Eastern Nigeria – a suspicion which far less attractive politicians than Eyo Ita fanned to red-hot virulence, and from which the Igbo have continued to reap enmity to this day.

I have gone on at such length on Dr Azikiwe and Chief Awolowo not because I have anything against them personally but because I believe quite strongly that if Nigeria is to avoid catastrophes of possibly greater dimensions than we have been through since Independence we must take a hard and unsentimental look at the crucial question of leadership and political power.

There is no doubt in my mind that the continued dominance of major areas of Nigerian politics by Azikiwe and Awolowo is of negative value. Not because they are old men now, but because their political thought which is the mainspring of political action was always at the best of times defective:

> henceforth I shall utilize my earned income to secure my enjoyment of a high standard of living and also . . . give a helping hand to the needy (Azikiwe)

> I was going to make myself formidable intellectually, morally invulnerable, to make all the money that is possible for a man with my brains and brawn to make in Nigeria (Awolowo)

Those were not the fireside musings in the evening of their lives but the youthful credo that launched and informed their political career. If we were a more discerning people we should not have trusted them with our lives even in the fifties and sixties.

But a much worse tragedy is looming over us. A crop

of newcomers in Nigerian politics emerged in 1979 whose manifest mission should have been to inaugurate a new philosophy and a new practice of politics devoid of narrowness and opportunism, and capable of preparing Nigeria in the twenty-odd years left of this century for the grim challenges of the Third Millenium. But they chose instead to become revivalists of a bankrupt and totally unusable tradition of political manouvering, tribal expediency and consummate selfishness. And they are valiantly fostering this diseased tradition among the masses of their followers by a soft-headed and patently dishonest adulation of a couple of tired old men who apparently see the Nigerian Presidency in the 1980s as a pension and gratuity for certain services they think they rendered to the nation thirty years ago.

Surely the electorate should find the courage to tell them that in as much as they have a right to dream their dreams of the past, they must not be allowed to block our vision of the present, or mortgage our children's chances of success in the twenty-first century.

I do not think that bad as it is our condition is totally bereft of hope or that our citizens are too dense to appreciate the explosive potentialities of the self-centred politics we practise.

Undoubtedly there are simply too many political actors on our stage whose prime purpose in grabbing power seems to be no higher than a desire to free themselves from every form of civilized restraint in their public and private lives.

But there is also in today's Nigerian social consciousness

a powerful impulse towards a new politics of peace and fair play. This impulse may be held temporarily in check by the dead grip of the patriarchs of an obsolescent dispensation. But the moment we can free our minds from their unwholesome spell a powerful ground swell which is gathering force even now will launch forth a generation of politicians able to respond appropriately to the challenge of our critical times.

Chief Obafemi Awolowo does have a reputation for seeking out and using talent, albeit to serve a narrow purpose. With the possible exception of the governor who saw nothing wrong in burying his father with public funds because the food and the wine provided were consumed by the people, Awolowo's team of state executives has men of undoubted ability. Bola Ige, however the 'political ebullition' of Oyo State may toss him around, is one of the brightest and most accomplished members of my generation. Bisi Onabanjo, whether or not he can contain the challenge of Ijebu traditionalism, is a brilliant and fearless journalist who, in my view, stands alone with Ernest Ikoli in the very pinnacle of his profession.

These and many others in their present narrow fraternity will emerge, one must hope, on a new and uncluttered national stage in genuine partnership with their fellows all over the country.

The case of Azikiwe's men will be somewhat different because he has never shown an excessive desire to surround himself with talent. In fairness though, it must be pointed out that he did not choose Jim Nwobodo; rather it was the other way round. But the cosy relationship that quickly developed between the old performer and the young genius of travesty leaves one in no doubt that no matter who originally chose whom the partnership could not have been more natural. The young, dashing governor may not have the master's powers of elocution; nor his taste and good breeding (for Zik would never have told a press conference, for instance, that he was not elected governor to carry shit!); but in other ways Jim seems an excellent apprentice. He worships publicity and uses the media with the insatiable greed of a born demagogue. In one issue alone of the government-owned *Daily Star* (January 3, 1980) there were *ten* pictures of Jim Nwobodo! In 1982 he spent tens of millions that could have paid his teachers' salaries to construct, in record time, the most modern television station in Black Africa. In his first term as Governor he has found it appropriate to build statues to himself. If he is aware of any conflict in combining high public office and the pursuit of private business his Administration is yet to reflect it.

Lately a new recruit to this camp has been the former fire-eating Abubakar Rimi of Kano State whose latest contribution to socialist thought in Nigeria was the statement that his party would win the votes of every Nigerian woman because of his handsomeness and the handsomeness of Jim Nwobodo!

The feudal insult to women aside, one must marvel at a situation in which a young, educated and articulate aspirant to state power and, above all, a recent follower of Mallam Aminu Kano, could find it in himself to trivialize and reduce national politics to the status of a beauty contest! (And wonder also where in this new political platform the handsome duet intends to hide poor Sam Mbakwe when the beauty parade begins!)

I can see no rational answer to the chaotic jumble of tragic and tragi-comical problems we have unleashed on ourselves in the past twenty-five years, but the example of Aminu Kano – a selfless commitment to the common people of our land whom we daily deprive and dispossess and whose plight we treat so callously and frivolously.

Aminu Kano had the imagination and intelligence to foresee the danger which our unjust social order poses for society and renounced the privilege of his class and identified himself completely through struggle with the fate of the down-trodden. When the late Prime Minister Abubakar Tafawa Balewa made the crack that if Aminu Kano were to become Prime Minister of Nigeria he would one day carry a placard and join a protest march against himself, he was paying a most profound and befitting tribute to a saint and revolutionary. He was extolling a mental and practical identification so complete and uncompromising that it could not be subverted, not even by the deadening blandishments of the highest office in the land. For it was indeed true that if for any reason Aminu Kano should discover that he had joined the ranks of the oppressor he would promptly and openly renounce his position and wage war on himself!

The importance to society of people like Aminu Kano or Mahatma Gandhi is not that every politician can become like them, for that would be an impossible and totally unrealistic expectation. But the monumental fact which they underscore and which no one can ignore again after they have walked among us is this: Gandhi was real; Aminu Kano was real. They were not angels in heaven, they were human like the rest of us, in India and Nigeria. Therefore, after their example, no one who reduces the high purpose of politics which they exemplified down to a swinish scramble can hope to do so without bringing a terrible judgement on himself.

Nigeria cannot be the same again because Aminu Kano lived here.